The Effects of Original Sin and the Availability of Sovereign Grace

by

David E. Bower

DORRANCE PUBLISHING CO., INC.
PITTSBURGH, PENNSYLVANIA 15222

All Rights Reserved
Copyright © 1996 by David E. Bower
No part of this book may be reproduced or transmitted in any form
or by any means, electronic or mechanical, including photocopying,
recording, or by any information storage and retrieval system
without permission in writing from the publisher.

ISBN # 0-8059-3871-0
Printed in the United States of America

First Printing

For more information or to order additional books, please write:
Dorrance Publishing Co., Inc.
643 Smithfield Street
Pittsburgh, Pennsylvania 15222
U.S.A.

To the memory of my son Timothy

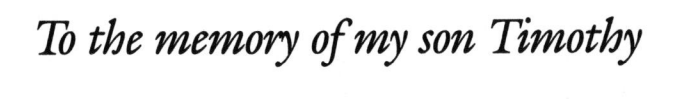

ACKNOWLEDGMENT

It is appropriate that I take this occasion to acknowledge my indebtedness to a multitude of acquaintances who in various ways have been a source of encouragement and inspiration to me and have thus contributed to the completion of this booklet. It is also appropriate that I acknowledge the good influence of my friend, David L. Painter, during the years when I attended his preaching services at the Reformed Baptist mission. The excellent presentation by Brother Painter of the doctrines of the Calvinist persuasion provided a source of enlightenment without which the writing of this booklet would have been much more difficult. It is also again appropriate that I should acknowledge the good influence of the preaching of numerous pastors of the Armenian persuasion. The enlightenment which their preaching provided, together with that of Brother Painter's preaching, provided an incentive which motivated me toward the conclusions at which I have arrived in the following pages. It is my hope and prayer that each reader will be comforted with the same comfort with which God has comforted me as He has illuminated the pages of the Bible for me.

David E. Bower

THE OBJECTIVE

It is hoped that the following pages will not be seen as an effort to blend the tenets of any of the various systems of theology to produce a more acceptable position on any one or more doctrinal declarations. It is hoped, rather, that the conclusions set forth in the following pages will be viewed as the product of careful examination of some doctrinal positions which have served to impede the proclamation and spread of the gospel. And further, it is hoped that the following pages will be found to reflect the scriptural view of the nature and character of God and of the race which He created in His own image. And finally it is hoped that the conclusions presented in the following pages will not be considered as an attack upon any system of doctrine, but rather, it is hoped that these conclusions will be useful to the adherents and proponents of every system of doctrine as they pursue the task of purifying and refining and perfecting those doctrinal heritages received from the past.

THE OVERVIEW

Offspring of Adam, born to die
Yet born to live with God on high
Recovered, though a fallen race
Redeemed alone by sovereign grace.

Not by wisdom of the mind
Not by mystic senses blind
Not by strong desire to find
Compelled by love, but not inclined.

You chose not Me, but I chose you,
Compelled not just a chosen few,
But mortals all, compelled to come,
Predestined all, and not just some.

David E. Bower
2980 Mickanin Rd.
N. Huntingdon, PA 15642

A REMONSTRANCE

If it should seem absurd for an unknown voice to question the conclusions of august theologians, then consider this: that although it has been often with good intentions, many knowledgeable theologians appear to have developed a disregard for some verities which are both eternal and absolute. By failing to recognize those verities which are both eternal and absolute and thus are the basis for sound theological conclusions, eternal truth has sometimes been made subservient to mental gymnastics and to the deficiencies of logic derived from tradition. The classic example is the advice given to Job by his three comforters. It is obvious from the experience of Job that philosophical reasoning is of little value in the arena of spiritual conflict. And a solution to the conflict between sin and grace is beyond the scope of philosophical reasoning. The following pages are presented with the intention of transcending philosophical reasoning by adhering to the absolutes of the Bible. The comments of the following pages have been limited to those aspects which have seemed to be the most basic and the most essential to a clear presentation of God's solution to the conflict between sin and grace.

THE EFFECTS OF ORIGINAL SIN AND THE AVAILABILITY OF SOVEREIGN GRACE

I. INTRODUCTION

Original sin is the term applied to the first sin committed by Adam and Eve in the garden of Eden and passed by God's sovereign decree upon all the descendants of Adam and Eve.

Original sin has been held as a basic doctrine by most churches. It has sometimes also been held that original sin resulted in spiritual death to the descendants of Adam and that recovery from the state of spiritual death is possible to only certain previously chosen persons.

It is the purpose of this paper to show from the scriptures that original sin is not the cause of spiritual death, and that God's sovereign grace, by which the righteousness of Christ is imputed to sinners as the only remedy for sin, is available to all who come to Him in repentance and faith.

Original sin, which is the sin of Adam which God imputes to all, is referred to by numerous scriptures. "In sin did my mother conceive me" the Psalmist declared in Psalm 51:5. Obviously there is no possibility of one committing sin at the very beginning of existence, that is, at the time of conception. Therefor the sin referred to above in Psalm 51:5 must be the sin of Adam which God imputes to all. It has been confirmed by many that all mortals bear the scar of Adam's sin. And further, Romans 3:9 confirms again that all of the descendants of Adam are conceived in sin.

Again, Romans 5:13 shows that it was only the first sin of Adam, which was committed while Adam and Eve were still in the garden of Eden, that could be then imputed to anyone. For "sin is not imputed when there is no law". And the only law, which was in effect from Adam to Moses, was the law forbidding them to eat of the tree of the knowledge of good and evil as described in Genesis 2:17. Adam and Eve sinned by violating that law and were then expelled from the garden of Eden. Nor was it possible for them or any of their descendants to enter that garden again. (Genesis 3:24) Thus their first sin could not be committed a second time.

And their first sin was the only sin which was forbidden by the law of God during the span of time from Adam to Moses. Therefor the first sin of Adam and Eve was the only sin which could be imputed to anyone during the span of time from Adam to Moses.

Romans 5:12-14 shows that death passed upon all men because of sin.

And as noted above, no sin except the first sin of Adam could be imputed to anyone during the time from Adam to Moses. Then the fact that death reigned over them all from Adam to Moses shows that Adam's first sin was indeed imputed to them all. For, until the time of Moses, no law existed as a basis for imputing any other sin, and it was "by sin" that death entered. (Romans 5:12)

II. THE REASON FOR IMPUTED SIN

The question may then arise: Why did God impute the sin of Adam to all? Such an act would ordinarily be unjust: to penalize someone for something which someone else had done. And if we view God's act of imputing the sin of Adam to all as an act separate and independent from all the other acts of God, then we would have to conclude that it was an unjust act indeed. But the scriptures should be sufficient to warn us that any view, which concludes that God acted unjustly, is in error. For Romans 9:14 tells us unrighteousness is not found in God. And further investigation will show that God did not impute the sin of Adam to all as an act separate and independent from all His other acts. But rather, God imputed the sin of Adam to all as an inseparable part of the complete plan for man's salvation. The imputed sin of Adam does not stand alone.

God imputed the sin of Adam to all "that He might have mercy upon all." (Romans 11:32 and Romans 5:18&19)

From Romans 11:32 it can be readily deducted that it was God's will to extend to all of the descendents of Adam and Eve the same mercy that He showed to Adam and Eve after they had sinned. But the descendents of Adam and Eve could not enter the garden of Eden as noted in Genesis 3:24. Therefore they could not commit the same sin (eating of the tree of the knowledge of good and evil) that Adam and Eve had committed. And since, until the time of Moses, there was no other law by which any sin could be imputed, then, before God could show mercy to the descendents of Adam, it was necessary for God to impute the sin of Adam to the descendents of Adam.

By imputing the sin of Adam to all, God did no injustice to the descendents of Adam. For God then imputed the righteousness of Christ to all, thus giving to every descendent of Adam more than that which could be taken away by the imputed sin of Adam. (Romans 5:18) And thus "where sin abounded, grace did much more abound." (Romans 5:20) When God imputed the sin of Adam to all of the descendents of Adam, all men became sinners, but they did not die spiritually. For God then imputed the righteousness of Christ to all (Romans 5:18) thus preventing spiritual death. And thus every descendent of Adam enters this life spiritually alive just as the apostle Paul said that he was spiritually alive (Romans 7:9) at some time previous to his conversion on the Damascus road. But the decree of physical death (Genesis 3:19) remained intact. And according to Romans 5:12-14 physical death is the visible confirmation that Adam's sin was imputed to every descendent of Adam.

And finally, it should be noted that, by imputing the sin of Adam to all, God set the stage to demonstrate that His grace is always sovereign. For God then demonstrated the sovereignty of His grace by imputing the righteousness of Christ as the remedy for the spiritual consequences of the imputed sin of Adam. And God's grace is sovereign, not only with respect to the imputed sin of Adam, but with respect to all sin. As it is for the imputed sin of Adam, so it is for the personal sin of any descendents of Adam. When God by His sovereign grace imputes the righteousness of Christ as the remedy for personal sin, that person is then spiritually alive. But God's condition must be met, and that condition is "repent ye, and believe the gospel". (Mark 1:15) But some refuse and die spiritually just as the apostle Paul died spiritually. (Romans 7:9) But God's sovereign grace is not defeated. For just as God compelled the apostle Paul to repent on the Damascus road, God will also compel every descendent of Adam to repent and believe the gospel even though they may have previously died spiritually.

III. THE REASON FOR IMPUTED RIGHTEOUSNESS

Once God had imputed the sin of Adam to all, it was then necessary to impute the righteousness of Christ to all to prevent spiritual death from occurring as a result of the imputed sin of Adam. This does not mean that God had created an emergency for which He had to find a solution. God knew what He would do about Adam's sin before He created Adam. But the reason why it was necessary to prevent spiritual death from resulting from the imputed sin of Adam was that His love for His creatures required it (Romans 5:8), and further, so that He would not be found unrighteous. For His word assures us of His righteousness (Daniel 9:14), and His acts never contradict His word. So to prevent His act (of imputing the sin of Adam to all) from contradicting His word, it was necessary for God to impute the righteousness of Christ to all. And that God did impute the righteousness of Christ to all is seen from Romans 5:18&19 and 1 Corinthians 15:22. And further, God imputed the sin of Adam to all so that He could impute the righteousness of Christ to all. Referring to the nation Israel, the apostle

Paul says in Romans 11:32, "For God hath concluded them all in unbelief, that He might have mercy upon all." And since God is no respecter of persons, all Gentiles would in like manner receive mercy. The 5th chapter of Romans gives a summary of the manner in which God triumphs over original sin. Three things presented in the 5th chapter of Romans establish the spiritual status of every descendant of Adam at the moment of conception:
1. The imputed sin of Adam. (Romans 5:12-14)
2. The imputed righteousness of Christ. (Romans 5:18)
3. The triumph of grace. (Romans 5:20)

God does not violate His principles of justice when He imputes the sin of Adam to each descendant of Adam. For God then imputes the righteousness of Christ to each descendant of Adam so that "where sin abounded, grace did much more abound". (Romans 5:20) God imputed the sin of Adam to all so that He could impute the righteousness of Christ to all. "For God hath concluded them all in unbelief, that He might have mercy upon all." (Romans 11:32) In triumphing over original sin God made each descendant of Adam a debtor to grace by giving to each descendant of Adam more by imputing the righteousness of Christ than could be taken away by the imputed sin of Adam.

That it was necessary for God to impute the righteousness of Christ to all may likewise be shown by the 18th chapter of Ezekiel. We should note first that this chapter is concerned with the spiritual consequences of sin. This is emphasized by the repeated declaration: "The soul that sinneth, it shall die.". (Ezekiel 18:4&20) (It should be noted that the reference here is not to an individual act of sin, but rather to choosing a life of sin.)

There are physical consequences of sin, and there are spiritual consequences of sin. Examination of the contexts of Ezekiel 18:20 and Exodus 34:7 indicates that Exodus 34:7 refers to the physical consequences of sin while Ezekiel 18:20 refers to the spiritual consequences of sin. And since "the son shall not bear the iniquity of the father." (Ezekiel 18:20), then obviously it was necessary for God to prevent the iniquity of the father (Adam) from resulting in adverse spiritual consequences to any of the descendants of Adam.

It is obvious from Romans 11:32 that it was necessary for God to impute the sin of Adam to all the descendants of Adam to accomplish His objective of showing mercy to all. And since "the wages of sin is death" (Romans 6:23), therefor it was necessary to supply a remedy for the imputed sin of Adam to prevent spiritual death from resulting to any of the descendants of Adam. And since the righteousness of Christ is the only remedy for sin, it was therefor necessary for God to impute the righteousness of Christ to all of the descendants of Adam. Thus God prevented spiritual death from resulting to any of the descendants of Adam as a consequence of the imputed sin of Adam. And thus the apostle, Paul, could say: "I was alive without the law once —". (Romans 7:9)

The question then arises: If a person is spiritually alive when he enters this world, then why is it necessary for him to be saved? To answer this question, it may be helpful to note that in the ability to procreate there was given, neither to Adam nor to any descendant of Adam, the ability to create a soul. The soul is the essential part of the person. This fact is reflected in the words of Eve after the birth of Cain when she said, "I have gotten a man from the Lord." (Genesis 4:1) God is actively involved in the propagation of the human race. By procreation and in accordance with the laws of nature which God established, man provides the physical body, and according to Genesis 2:7 and Ecclesiastics 12:7, God provides the soul.

And to conclude that the souls which God creates are spiritually dead is unreasonable, for Paul declared that, at sometime previous to his Damascus road experience, he was spiritually alive. (Romans 7:9) And to be spiritually alive before the conversion experience, a person must be spiritually alive when he is born into this earthly life. Not only is this conclusion in harmony with the Scriptures; the Scriptures allow for no other conclusion.

For if a person is spiritually dead, he can become spiritually alive only by a conversion experience. And the 6th chapter of Hebrews shows conclusively that the conversion experience cannot occur more than once in any person's life. If Paul had been spiritually dead when he came into this world, then to become spiritually alive (as he said he was in Romans 7:9) he would have had to have a conversion experience. If he had had a conversion experience to become spiritually alive, then he could not have died spiritually, as he said that he did (Romans 7:9). Nor could he have had a second conversion experience, for according to the 6th chapter of Hebrews, the conversion experience is permanent. It is permanent because it is impossible to fall away, for to fall away would result in crucifying Christ again. And according to Romans 6:9, it is impossible to crucify Christ again. This is God's safeguard to our salvation.

When the righteousness of Christ is imputed to any person, that person is then spiritually alive. Paul was spiritually alive as he said in Romans 7:9. However it is necessary to determine whether the righteousness of Christ was first imputed to Paul at the time of conception or at a later time in his life. If it is assumed that Paul was spiritually dead when he came into this world, then to become spiritually alive (as he said he was at some time previous to his conversion experience on the Damascus road) Paul would have had to have a conversion experience previous to his conversion experience on the Damascus road. And this would be impossible, for according to Hebrews 6:4-6, the conversion experience is permanent, and thus a person can have only one conversion experience. And since the only way a spiritually dead person can become spiritually alive is by a conversion experience, and since Paul's Damascus road conversion experience eliminated the possibility that Paul had a previous conversion experience, then it follows that Paul was spiritually alive when he came into this world. And thus the righteousness of Christ was imputed to Paul at the time of conception thus preventing spiritual death from occurring as a result of the imputed sin of Adam. And as it was with Paul, so it is with every descendant of Adam. God brought Paul into this world spiritually alive, and likewise God brings every person into this world spiritually alive. "For there is no respect of persons with God. (Romans 2:11).

And although a person is born spiritually alive, yet he does sin, and therefor he must repent and trust in Christ to save him from impending spiritual death. When the Holy Spirit convicts a person "of sin, and of righteousness, and of judgment" (John 16:8), that person then is confronted with the command of Jesus: "Repent ye and believe the gospel.". (Mark 1:15) Paul was spiritually alive when he was confronted with this commandment. In Romans 7:9 Paul relates how he died spiritually: "For I was alive without the law once: but when the commandment came, sin revived, and I died.". If Paul had obeyed "the commandment" (Repent ye, and believe the gospel"), he would have remained spiritually alive. Likewise any person who is confronted for the first time with the commandment ("Repent ye, and believe the gospel.") will remain spiritually alive if he obeys the commandment. When a person obeys the command to repent and believe the gospel, this constitutes a conversion experience. And as noted above, after any person has had a conversion experience, it is impossible for that person to die spiritually. Also, if a person rejects the command to repent and believe the gospel and consequently dies spiritually and then at a later time obeys that command, this also constitutes a conversion experience, and thereafter that person cannot die spiritually. Also, it can be further stated that, since God "now commandeth all men everywhere to repent" (Acts 17:30), it is impossible for anyone to reach the hypothetical point described in Hebrews 6:4-6 at which point repentance is impossible. This again emphasizes the fact that it is impossible for anyone who has had a conversion experience to fall away and lose his salvation.

The preceding statements relating to whether or not a person is spiritually alive at birth can be illustrated by letting a straight line represent the length of the life of the Apostle Paul. Let the left hand end (1) of the line represent the time of Paul's birth, and let the right hand end (5) of the line represent the time of Paul's death. Then let the length of time that Paul was spiritually alive before he died spiritually (Romans 7:9) be represented by (2), and let the point at which Paul died spiritually be represented by (3). And let the point in time of Paul's Damascus road conversion be represented by (4).

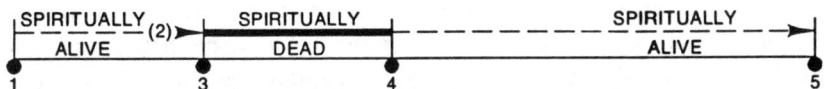

In conclusion, if Paul had been spiritually dead when he was born, then he could have become spiritually alive (2) only by a conversion experience. If he had had a conversion experience to become spiritually alive (2), then he could not have died spiritually (3). The condition and events described in Romans 7:9 could not have occurred after Paul's Damascus road conversion experience (4) since spiritual death cannot occur after conversion. Therefor the condition and events of Romans 7:9 had to have occurred before Paul's Damascus road conversion (4). And further, since Paul did die spiritually (3), (Romans 7:9), then it is obvious that he did not become spiritually alive (2) as the result of a conversion experience. And since there is no other way whereby Paul could have become spiritually alive (2), then it is obvious that he was spiritually alive when he was born. And since "God is no respecter of persons: (Acts 10:34), then every descendent of Adam is spiritually alive when born into this world.

IV. THE REASON FOR PHYSICAL DEATH

But while God prevented spiritual death by imputing the righteousness of Christ to all, His plan of salvation did provide for instituting physical death. And God chose to decree physical death to reign from Adam's time to the present, as the scripture states in Hebrews 9:27 "— it is appointed unto men once to die —".

But if God supplied a remedy for the imputed sin of Adam, why then do men die? This question may be answered by noting that the atoning blood of Christ cleanses the soul, but it does not cleanse the physical body. And when the atoning blood of Christ is applied to the soul, the righteousness of Christ is imputed to that soul. Thus that soul is redeemed, but the redemption of the body is accomplished thru physical death. (Romans 8:23 &

1 Corinthians 15:36)

The physical body is corrupted by the imputed sin of Adam. Physical death is not caused by the imputed sin of Adam, but rather physical death is the remedy by which the "corruption" (1 Corinthians 15:42), resulting from the imputed sin of Adam, is eliminated.

The reason for physical death can be determined first by noting two reasons why physical death could not have been caused by the sin of Adam.

The first reason is that Adam and Eve did not die physically in the day in which they sinned in the garden of Eden. For since God said: "In the day that thou eatest thereof thou shalt surely die.", and since they did not die physically in the day that they sinned by eating of the tree of the knowledge of good and evil, then it is obvious that it was spiritual death that was specified in Genesis 2:17. And that Adam and Eve did die spiritually is indicated by the fact that they hid themselves from the Lord as noted in Genesis 3:8.

The second reason is that the consequence of sin can only be nullified by "the Lamb of God which taketh away the sin of the world." (John 1:29) Therefor the tree of life could not nullify the consequence of sin; the tree of life could, however, nullify physical death. Therefor physical death could not be the consequence of sin. The physical consequences of the first sin of Adam are the imperfections and frailties and distortions seen throughout the whole physical creation which creation was previously perfect when created. All creation suffered by the first sin of Adam as described in Romans 8:22, "For we know that the whole creation groaneth and travaileth in pain together until now.". Then Romans 8:23 goes on to explain that also our physical bodies are subjected to the adverse physical consequences of the first sin of Adam and also that we wait for "the redemption of our body." And, as explained in 1 Corinthians 15:36 and 44, "the redemption of our body" is accomplished through physical death. But death does not provide "the redemption of the body." It should be noted that death is an "enemy." (1 Corinthians 15:26) Yet God decrees death to overtake us in order that the stage might be set for us to receive a spiritual body. (1 Corinthians 15:44) The greatest physical tragedy is not death. The greater tragedy would be to live forever in a physical world corrupted by the first sin of Adam and with a physical body also corrupted by the first sin of Adam. It was to prevent this tragedy that God drove Adam from the garden of Eden: "lest he put forth his hand, and take also of the tree of life, and eat, and live forever." (Genesis 3:22) But it should be noted that the painful and sometimes terrifying aspects of physical death serve as a warning to man not to attempt to enter the chambers of death by using his own devices to hasten the hour of death. It remains then that physical death was ordained by the decree of

God stated in Genesis 3:19 "dust thou art, and unto dust shalt thou return.".

Physical death is by the appointment of God. "It is appointed unto men once to die." (Hebrews 9:27) But spiritual death is the consequence of sin, and at least one further observation is necessary regarding the reason for physical death.

To what end did God ordain physical death? Before attempting to answer this question, it may be helpful to note that after Adam and Eve sinned, God first provided to Adam and Eve the remedy for spiritual death which remedy was symbolized by the "coats of skins". (Genesis 3:21) With Adam and Eve thus restored to spiritual life, God then drove them out of the garden of Eden to prevent them from eating of the tree of life. And so this guaranteed that the decree of physical death (Genesis 3:19) would remain intact.

It may also be helpful to note that the decree of spiritual death (Genesis 2:17) was absolute without exception. But the decree of Genesis 3:19 obviously referred to the termination of physical life without specifying how that termination would occur thus allowing Enoch and Elijah to leave this world without falling asleep in death, and also to allow for those saints who on some future day will be caught up together with the resurrected dead "to meet the Lord in the air". (1 Thessalonians 4:17) For it was not the effects of the imputed sin of Adam that brought Enoch and Elijah to that terminal point where the dust returns to the earth as described in Ecclesiastics 12:7. It was God who brought Enoch and Elijah to that terminal point. And these examples show clearly that physical death is not caused by the imputed sin of Adam.

Neither was physical death decreed as punishment for personal sin as can be seen in the case of an infant who dies a few moments after being born. The infant did not sin but nevertheless died physically. Personal sin, as in the case of the disobedient prophet, in 1 Kings 13:26, may sometimes hasten physical death. Or the intervention of God, as in the case of Hezekiah (Isaiah 38:5), may delay the time of physical death. But regardless of personal sin or righteousness, physical death occurs because "it is appointed unto men once to die". (Hebrews 9:27) And that appointment is certain even with the intervention of God as in the cases of Enoch and Elijah and those saints who will be alive and remaining on the resurrection day. For while Enoch and Elijah did not sleep the sleep of death, it seems necessary to conclude that they did fulfill their appointment with death as described in Ecclesiastics 12:7. For "flesh and blood cannot inherit the kingdom of God." (1 Corinthians 15:50)

For death as referred to in Hebrews 9:27 is the terminal point at which "the spirit shall return unto God who gave it" (Ecclesiastics 12:7), and it is also at that same terminal point that the dust returns "to the earth as it was.". (Ecclesiastics 12:7) Death is that point at which the soul terminates its residence in the mortal physical body. And while death may be hastened as a form of punishment, it will also be the termination point at which all of the grief and pain, which so often distresses every mortal, will be exchanged for joy and peace in the presence of the Lord.

And again to better understand the nature of physical death, we may ponder whether the spirit returns "unto God who gave it" because the physical body is no longer a fit habitation for the soul. Or we may also ponder whether the physical body ceases to function because the spirit has returned "unto God who gave it". (Ecclesiastics 12:7)

And further, we may ponder whether or not Enoch and Elijah received their spiritual bodies when their physical lives were terminated. The fact that Moses and Elijah were visible to Peter, James and John on the Mount of Transfiguration (Luke 9:32) seems to indicate that Moses and Elijah did receive temporary spiritual bodies at the termination of their physical lives. And the fact that Moses physical life was terminated at a time of robust health (Deuteronomy 34:7), and the fact that Moses was buried by God and "no man knoweth of his sepulchre", (Deuteronomy 34:6) and the fact that Moses pleased God (Deuteronomy 34:10) present enough resemblance to Enoch to allow for the possibility that Enoch may also have received a temporary spiritual body when translated. And the miraculous nature of the termination of the physical lives of Enoch and Moses and Elijah provide a graphic presentation of the resurrection morning when "we shall all be changed" (1 Corinthians 15:51) and receive a "spiritual body". (1 Corinthians 15:44)

Also, it is obvious from the context immediately following verse 51, that the theory that the first resurrection will occur in two or more phases is unscriptural. For the duration of the first resurrection is limited to "the twinkling of an eye" (verse 52), and it is definitely specified that the first resurrection will occur "at the last trump". (verse 52) (See also 1 Thessalonians 4:16 and Revelation 11:15) And since "all" will be changed at the same moment, then the first resurrection must take place after the death of the last martyr of the great tribulation. For "we shall all be changed" (verse 51), includes all the martyrs of the great tribulation. (Revelation 6:11)

But it is certain that a terminal point exists where the dust returns to earth and the spirit returns to God who gave it. Enoch did not experience the process of physical death as mortals normally do. But there was of necessity a terminal point when Enoch was translated. And at that terminal point Enoch's physical body returned to the earth, and his spirit returned to "God who gave it." (Ecclesiastes 12:7) For, as noted above, "flesh and blood cannot inherit the kingdom of God." (1 Corinthians 15:50) Enoch was not acquainted with death in that he did not experience death as other mortals did during the span of time from Adam to Moses. But Enoch did fulfill his appointment with death when he reached that terminal point described in Ecclesiastics 12:7 — "Then shall the dust return to the earth as it was: and the spirit shall return unto God who gave it." For according to Romans 5:14 everyone from Adam until the time of Moses fulfilled the appointment with death. (Genesis 3:19, Ecclesiastics 12:7, and Hebrews 9:27)

And the translation of Enoch shows that physical death is not caused by the imputed sin of Adam. By translating Enoch, God Himself brought Enoch to that terminal point where the body returns to earth and the spirit returns to God. It was not the imputed sin of Adam nor was it personal sin that brought Enoch to that terminal point.

From these observations then, it may be concluded that neither personal sin nor the imputed sin of Adam were the basic reason for the decree of physical death. While personal sin does often hasten the hour of physical death, and while God may punish a person by hastening the time of physical death (e.g. the requirement by God in Genesis 9:6 of the death penalty for murder), yet physical death itself was not decreed as punishment for either personal sin or for the imputed sin of Adam.

The answer, then, to the question (to what end did God ordain physical death?) is found in the words from Romans 8:23 "— the redemption of our body.". And to confirm this we may refer to the 15th chapter of 1 Corinthians, verse 36, "— that which thou sowest is not quickened, except it die.". Verse 44 tells us further that "it is sown a natural body; it is raised a spiritual body." Thus physical death was decreed so that we might receive a spiritual body in the resurrection in harmony with Revelation 21:5 when He who sits upon the throne says, "Behold, I make all things new.".

So then the decree of physical death will have served its purpose, and "the redemption of our body" will be complete as described in 1 Corinthians 15:54, "So when this corruptible shall have put on incorruption, and this mortal shall have put on immortality, then shall be brought to pass the saying that is written, Death is swallowed up in victory".

V. THE CAUSE OF SPIRITUAL DEATH

With the reason for physical death clarified, the cause of spiritual death can be more readily understood. And it should be noted before proceeding further, that, while physical death has a definite purpose, spiritual death has no purpose. Physical death is a part of God's complete plan of salvation. Spiritual death made the plan of salvation necessary. God drove Adam and Eve out of the garden of Eden to guarantee that the decree of physical death would remain in effect. But God sent His Son to provide the remedy for spiritual death. And when Jesus Christ died on the cross, He provided the remedy which can restore to spiritual life those who have died spiritually.

It was previously noted that spiritual death is the consequence of sin. Also, it was previously shown that spiritual death is not the consequence of the imputed sin of Adam. Spiritual death then is caused by personal sin. So it is necessary to determine what specific personal sin causes spiritual death.

To this end the experience of the apostle, Paul, may be considered. In Romans 7:9 Paul tells how he came to die spiritually: "For I was alive without the law once: but when the commandment came, sin revived, and I died.".

It is sometimes assumed that the commandment referred to in Romans 7:9 is the same commandment listed in Romans 7:7, "Thou shall not covet.". But nowhere in scripture does it state that this commandment carries the penalty of spiritual death.

But the commandment of Jesus in Mark 1:15 does carry the penalty of spiritual death. And that commandment is "Repent ye, and believe the gospel.". The warning that spiritual death occurs as a result of disobeying this commandment is found first in Luke 13:3&5 where Jesus says "Except ye repent, ye shall all likewise perish", and again in John 3:18 where Jesus says that "he that believeth not is condemned already.".

And it may be noted further from the scriptures that it is not possible for any other commandment to carry the penalty of spiritual death. For when a person obeys the command to repent and believe the gospel, he passes a point of no return. It is impossible for him to return to that place in time where he formerly could have disobeyed the commandment of Jesus to repent and believe the gospel. Because, when a person obeys the command to repent and believe the gospel, at that instant, he receives the gift of eternal life. (See 1 John 5:11-13) When the gift of eternal life is given, the person to whom it is given is changed forever and cannot die spiritually. For eternal life is eternal.

An analysis of Paul's experience in Romans 7:9 indicates the following:

1. "The commandment" was one specific commandment and only one, no more.

2. "The commandment" applies universally to every descendant of Adam. From Paul's words, "when the commandment came", it appears obvious that he is implying what is confirmed by Acts 17:30 that the same

"commandment" which came to Paul also comes to every person.

3. Since it is referred to as "the commandment" this suggests that it is of greater importance than any other commandment. This is confirmed by the fact that rejecting this commandment resulted in the most severe spiritual consequence, spiritual death, for Paul.

4. That Paul is referring to the same commandment given by the Lord Jesus in Mark 1:15 is confirmed by the fact that the consequence of rejecting the command to repent and believe the gospel is spiritual death as noted in Luke 13:3&5 and John 3:36.

5. Obeying "the commandment" to repent and believe the gospel is the only means of avoiding spiritual death.

The essential message of the Bible emphasizes the eternal benefits of saving faith and the dismal consequences of refusing to repent and believe the gospel. And further, while disobeying the commandment (repent ye and believe the gospel) is the only cause of spiritual death, it should also be noted that the only requirement for recovering from spiritual death is to obey that same commandment.

It is significant that Jesus launched His earthly ministry with the commandment "repent ye, and believe the gospel" (Mark 1:15) and concluded His earthly ministry by offering Himself upon the cross for the purpose of providing the gift of eternal life to all who obey that same commandment. No other commandment qualifies to be referred to as "the commandment". For "repent ye, and believe the gospel" is the only commandment which, if obeyed, carries the promise of eternal life and which, if rejected, carries the penalty of spiritual death.

VI. THE RELATION OF SPIRITUAL DEATH TO THE BLASPHEMY AGAINST THE HOLY GHOST

It has been supposed that in some cases recovery from spiritual death is impossible because of the wording of those scriptures which deal with the blasphemy against the Holy Ghost. (Matthew 12:22-32; Mark 3:22-30; Luke 12:10) These scriptures appear to contradict the conclusion that the only cause of spiritual death is disobeying the command to repent and believe the gospel. Therefor it is necessary to determine where the misunderstanding is, for there are no contradictions in the holy scriptures.

This problem can be solved by determining first, what offence was the cause of the blasphemy against the Holy Ghost, and second, whether that blasphemy would never be forgiven. It should be observed that, previous to the incident recorded in Matthew 12:22-32 and Mark 3:22-30, there is no indication that the consequence of blasphemy against the Holy Ghost would be spiritual death. And since "sin is not imputed when there is no law" (Romans 5:13), then it can be concluded that the reckless words of those scribes and Pharisees ("He hath Beelzebub, and by the prince of devils casteth He out devils.") was not what put those scribes and Pharisees "in danger of eternal damnation". (Mark 3:29)

But when those scribes and Pharisees said NO to the gracious invitation of the Holy Ghost to obey the commandment (Repent ye, and believe the gospel.) (Mark 1:15), they died spiritually. For they were then guilty of violating a law which did already exist: "he that believeth not is condemned already, because he hath not believed in the name of the only begotten Son of God." (John 3:18)

Their offence was the refusal to believe, but Jesus showed that unbelief was related to the blasphemy against the Holy Ghost. Those scribes and Pharisees died spiritually, not because of blasphemy against the Holy Ghost, but because of refusing to repent and believe the gospel. Their reckless words in Mark 3:22 gives evidence of their unbelief.

The nature of the blasphemy against the Holy Ghost can be seen more clearly by noting the reason why the sin of blasphemy is mentioned. When Jesus directed the attention of those scribes and Pharisees to their offence, He was calling attention to the evidence of their unbelief. By reminding them that their refusal to believe resulted in blasphemy against the Holy Ghost, Jesus was showing them that their offence was infinitely more serious than any attempt to silence or discredit Him. By showing them that, when they were attempting to discredit Him and thus openly displaying their refusal to believe, they were in reality also speaking against or blaspheming against the Holy Ghost, Jesus is emphasizing the deadly nature of their refusal to believe.

The fact that they attempted to discredit Jesus is positive evidence of their refusal to believe. And the fact that they attempted to discredit Jesus by saying "He hath Beelzebub, and by the prince of devils casteth He out devils" is unquestionably blasphemy against the Holy Ghost. First, the scribes and Pharisees refused to repent and believe. And then, in attempting to justify their refusal to repent and believe, they blasphemed against the Holy Ghost. But since their refusal to believe rendered them spiritually dead immediately, then to specify any penalty for blasphemy against the Holy Ghost would have served no purpose. For the penalty for unbelief was already prescribed in John 3:18.

Additional light may be cast upon this dark subject by referring to the essential message of Jesus in Mark 1:15, "— the kingdom of God is at hand:

repent ye, and believe the gospel.". When Jesus said, "the kingdom of God is at hand," He also stated the unchanging requirements for entrance into His kingdom. This is essentially the same as His statement in Matthew 12:28, "the kingdom of God is come unto you.". The message that those scribes and Pharisees heard that day, and doubtless previously, was essentially the same as Jesus proclaimed at the beginning of His ministry: "— the kingdom of God is at hand: repent ye, and believe the gospel.".

But when Jesus said, "if I cast out devils by the Spirit of God, then the kingdom of God is come unto you." (Matthew 12:28), He was also emphasizing that it was by the Spirit of God that He preached the kingdom of God. The Holy Ghost was actively present in all of the healing and teaching and preaching ministry of Jesus. For, since Jesus did cast out devils by the Spirit of God, it is obvious that the Holy Spirit would be actively present in the preaching ministry of Jesus. For, since the Holy Ghost was actively present in the realm of physical healing, He would be no less actively present in the realm of spiritual healing.

The Holy Ghost was inseparable from the total ministry of Jesus. Therefor when those scribes and Pharisees blasphemed against Jesus, they also blasphemed against the Holy Ghost. When those scribes and Pharisees said that Jesus cast out devils "by Beelzebub the prince of devils" (Matthew 12:24), they clearly blasphemed against the Holy Ghost.

And while the offence of those scribes and Pharisees was designated as blasphemy against the Holy Ghost, yet as described in Matthew 12:22-32 and Mark 3:22-30, this same offence is also blasphemy against the Son. Thus forgiveness for this same offence is offered, for blasphemy against the Son "shall be forgiven". (Matthew 12:32) Jesus was not establishing a point of no return beyond which salvation is impossible. But rather Jesus was warning those Pharisees and scribes that they could not be restored to spiritual life except by obeying the commandment of Jesus to repent and believe the gospel. (See Mark 1:15) The offence described (in Matthew 12:22-32) as blasphemy against the Holy Ghost is also, first of all, blasphemy directed specifically against Jesus, the Son. Blasphemy against the Son is forgiven (See Matthew 12:32), and since it is here the same offence which is referred to in Matthew 12:31 as blasphemy against the Holy Ghost, then blasphemy against the Holy Ghost is forgiven, but not by the Holy Ghost. Forgiveness is the function of God the Father (See Luke 23:34) and of God the Son (See Mark 2:5-11). Forgiveness is not the function of the Holy Ghost, but rather, the Holy Ghost testifies of the forgiveness which Christ offers (See John 15:26 and Romans 8:16). And as Charles Wesley so eloquently wrote:

> *The Father hears Him pray,*
> *His dear anointed One;*
> *He cannot turn away,*
> *The presence of His Son:*
> *His Spirit answers to the blood,*
> *And tells me I am born of God.*

And it should be noted further that there is no evidence to indicate that forgiveness is withheld as a penalty for either the blasphemy against the Holy Ghost or for the refusal to believe. But since the refusal to believe results in spiritual death, forgiveness would accomplish nothing. The word "forgiveness", as used in the verses dealing with the blasphemy against the Holy Ghost, comes from the Greek word "aphiemi" which means "to send away". But since spiritual death occurred, then to send away the cause of spiritual death would not restore the spiritual corpse to spiritual life again. The remedy for spiritual death is to be born of the Spirit.

Forgiveness would serve no purpose before the work of grace is done. Nor will a sinner call upon God before the work of grace is done. When a sinner calls upon God for forgiveness, this is an identifying proof of the conversion experience.

Forgiveness is reserved for those who are spiritually alive and for no others. Spiritual life is restored to those who have died spiritually when they repent and believe in the name of the only begotten Son of God. And when they are spiritually alive, then forgiveness follows. But as long as a person continues to blaspheme against the Holy Ghost, thus demonstrating unbelief, that person remains spiritually dead, and forgiveness is not supplied "to send away" his sins.

For the blasphemy against the Holy Ghost is not only one act, but also a continuing activity, resulting from refusal to believe. Unbelief perpetuates spiritual death and keeps the blasphemer "in danger of eternal damnation". (Mark 3:29) And as long as he continues to blaspheme against the Holy Ghost, he stills remains unforgiven. (Mark 3:29) But when the refusal to believe gives way to faith, then God's restoring grace fills the life with joy and peace in the Holy Ghost.

To show that restoration to spiritual life and also complete forgiveness is possible after a person has blasphemed against the Holy Ghost, it must be recognized that blasphemy against Christ is also blasphemy against the Holy Ghost. It is clear from 2 Timothy 3:16, 2 Peter 1:20&21 and John 15:26 and 16:8 that the Holy Ghost testifies that the scriptural record is true and that Christ is both sinless and perfect. Thus anyone who speaks against or blasphemes against Christ is declaring that the Holy Ghost is a liar when the Holy Ghost testifies that Christ is sinless and perfect. And to declare that the Holy Ghost is a liar most certainly is blasphemy against the Holy Ghost. Therefor anyone who blasphemes against Christ also blasphemes against the Holy Ghost. Again it can be seen in Matthew 12:22-32 and in Mark 3:22-30 that, although the blasphemy of those Pharisees and scribes was directed against Jesus, yet their blasphemy was also against the Holy Ghost. And since Jesus said, "I and My Father are One", then it must follow that any blasphemy against Jesus is also against the Father and hence against all three Persons of the Trinity. These observations, then, lead to the conclusion that all blasphemy against God is against all three Persons of the Trinity. For to blaspheme against any one Person of the Trinity is to blaspheme against God. And since God is three Persons, then to blaspheme against God is to blaspheme against all three Persons of the Trinity. The perfect harmony and unity and equality which exists in the Trinity is the basis for this conclusion. And while blasphemy against the Holy Ghost is not forgiven by the Holy Ghost, yet because it is the same offence as blasphemy against the Son, then this same offence not only can be forgiven, but "shall be forgiven". (Matthew 12:32 & Mark 3:28) And thus restoration to spiritual life and also complete forgiveness is possible after a person has blasphemed against the Holy Ghost. But the Holy Ghost does not forgive sins. "The Spirit and the bride say, Come." (Revelation 22:17) But neither the Spirit nor the bride offer forgiveness. But the Spirit and the bride extend the invitation to come to "the Lamb of God which taketh away the sin of the world." (John 1:29)

And herein is the character of the Holy Ghost magnified in that He restores spiritual life to those who have died spiritually even though they have blasphemed against Him after saying NO to His gracious invitation to repent and believe. And there is no clearer example of this in scripture than the transformation of that blasphemer and chief of sinners, Saul of Tarsus, on the Damascus road. Having died spiritually some time previously (Romans 7:9), we see him restored to spiritual life and chosen to the high office of Apostle to the Gentiles.

And the extent to which the Holy Ghost worked in and through the Apostle Paul, to establish the church and to provide the inspired epistles to nurture the church throughout this age of grace, further confirms the gracious character of the Holy Ghost in a brilliance of glory unsurpassed. And also, the perfect unity and harmony and equality that exists among the three Persons of the Trinity leaves no room for any conclusion contrary to this: That the Holy Ghost is a God of love no less than the Father and the Son.

And far from declaring that sovereign grace is no longer available to those who have blasphemed against the Holy Ghost, the Scriptures show rather that God places no limitation on the availability of sovereign grace to all those who repent and believe the gospel.

VII. THE NATURE OF SPIRITUAL DEATH

Having established that recovery from spiritual death is possible for all who have died spiritually, it is appropriate to review briefly the nature of spiritual death and to probe further into the effects of original sin and the availability of sovereign grace.

It was previously noted that the wording of Psalm 51:5 indicates that the sin of Adam is imputed at the moment of conception. And since Romans 5:12-14 and Romans 11:32 show that the sin of Adam is imputed to all, and since Romans 5:18 and Romans 11:32 show that the righteousness of Christ is imputed to all, it is then necessary to conclude that God always imputes the righteousness of Christ immediately after the sin of Adam is imputed to eliminate the possibility of any adverse spiritual effect which would result from the imputed sin of Adam.

For since, "the son shall not bear the iniquity of the father" (Ezekiel 18:20), then there must be no lapse of time after the sin of Adam is imputed until the righteousness of Christ is imputed. For otherwise, during that lapse of time, God's guarantee, that "the son shall not bear the iniquity of the father" (Ezekiel 18:20), would be rendered void. Therefor since the sin of Adam is imputed at the moment of conception, and since there is no lapse of time until the righteousness of Christ is imputed, then beginning at conception every person is spiritually alive. And thus it is clear that spiritual death is not caused by the imputed sin of Adam. This is confirmed by the apostle, Paul, in Romans 7:9 where he says: "For I was alive without the law once: but when the commandment came, sin revived, and I died.".

That spiritual death is not caused by the imputed sin of Adam is shown again when Jesus confirms that all are spiritually alive when they are born into this earthly life. For when referring to little children in Mark 10:14, Jesus said: "of such is the kingdom of God.".

Again, it is established by the scriptures that spiritual death is not a consequence of the imputed sin of Adam. For as noted previously in Ezekiel 18:4&20, spiritual death is caused by personal sin. And again as noted previously, only one personal sin can cause spiritual death, and that sin is the refusal to repent and believe the gospel. "— Repent ye, and believe the gospel," is the commandment which was intended to preserve spiritual life (Romans 7:10), and was "the commandment" the rejection of which resulted in spiritual death for Paul. (Romans 7:9-11)

That "the commandment" of Romans 7:9 differs from all other commandments of God may be further confirmed by observing the nature of a familiar promise: "If we confess our sins, He is faithful and just to forgive us our sins, and to cleanse us from all unrighteousness." (1 John 1:9) From this promise, it is safe to conclude that God will forgive any truly converted person of any sin committed if that person confesses that sin to God. However there is one sin which results in spiritual death thus eliminating the possibility of forgiveness as offered in 1 John 1:9. And that sin is the rejection of the command to repent and believe the gospel. (Mark 1:15) And as noted previously, that sin cannot be committed after a person has had a conversion experience.

And there are two reasons why there is no promise of forgiveness to anyone who has refused to repent and believe. The first reason is that rejection of the command to repent and believe the gospel results immediately in spiritual death as in the case of Paul in Romans 7:9. And since the promise of forgiveness in 1 John 1:9 is made only to those who have been converted, the person who is spiritually dead is not included in this promise. The second reason why there is no promise of forgiveness is that the spiritually dead person will remain spiritually dead until he obeys the command to repent and believe the gospel. God has decreed in Luke 13:3&5 and in John 3:18 that he will remain spiritually dead until he does repent and believe the gospel.

Thus it can be seen that the command to repent and believe the gospel is in a category all by itself. For it is the only commandment which, if rejected, results in spiritual death and which, if obeyed, carries the promise of eternal life.

However, on the basis of 1 John 3:15 the question may arise as to whether a person who commits murder does not also die spiritually as the result of committing murder. To answer the question, it should first be noted that this scripture does not say anything about the <u>cause</u> of spiritual death. But rather it is the <u>evidence</u> of spiritual death as well as the <u>evidence</u> of spiritual life that is discussed in the 3rd chapter of 1 John. But the scripture presents the conclusive answer in the 14th verse: "He that loveth not his brother abideth in death.". Obviously a person would cease to love his brother before he murdered his brother. And since the scripture says in verse 14 that a person is already spiritually dead when he ceases to love his brother, then he is certainly spiritually dead before he murders his brother. So murder is not the cause of spiritual death; the cause is rejection of the command to repent and believe the gospel. And for those who do die spiritually, the only remedy is to obey the command to repent and believe the gospel.

To emphasize once more that the imputed sin of Adam does not cause spiritual death, we must pursue the scriptures further. And first we must be able to conclude that the scriptures do declare that it was the first sin of Adam alone by which "death passed upon all men." (Romans 5:12) By considering only that period of time which extended from Adam to Moses, the possibility of death entering by any other cause is eliminated for the following reasons:

1. Death was decreed because of sin of some kind. (Genesis 3:19 & Romans 5:12)

2. There are two categories of sin from Adam to Moses:

    a. Adam's first sin which was specifically prohibited by the law of God in Genesis 2:17.

    b. All the rest of the sins of Adam, none of which were prohibited by any law of God, and also all of the sins of all the descendants of Adam which sins also were not at that time prohibited by any law of God, for at that time the only law that had been given was the law forbidding Adam and Eve to eat of the fruit of the tree of the knowledge of good and evil. (Genesis 2:17)

3. Because "sin is not imputed when there is no law" (Romans 5:13) therefor none of the sins included in (2b) above were imputed to Adam or to any of his descendants during the time from Adam to Moses.

4. Therefor, the only sin which could be imputed to Adam or to his descendants was Adam's first sin.

5. And further, since Adam's first sin was the only sin that could be imputed to anyone, it was the only sin which could be the means by which death entered.

6. To eliminate the physical results of the first sin of Adam was the reason for the decree of physical death for Adam. (Genesis 3:19) (1 Corinthians 15:42&44)

7. And finally, that Adam's first sin was imputed to all the descendants of Adam is evident. For death did not enter by any other means. And since "death passed upon all men" (Romans 5:12), this showed that Adam's first sin had indeed been imputed to all the descendants of Adam without exception. And even Enoch of Genesis 5:24 fulfilled his appointment with death, although, as noted previously, he did not sleep the sleep of death. And since the sin of Adam is imputed to all of the descendants of Adam without exception, it is then possible to determine what kind of death is referred to in Romans 5:12.

To this end what the scriptures say about John the Baptist may be considered. For although the sin of Adam was imputed to John the Baptist, yet we know that he was born spiritually alive, for the prophecy in Luke 1:15 said "— he shall be filled with the Holy Ghost, even from his mother's womb." Thus the imputed sin of Adam did not cause John the Baptist to die spiritually. But we know from Matthew 14:10 that John the Baptist did die physically. Thus Romans 5:12 refers only to physical death. However, physical death is not caused by the imputed sin of Adam.

But physical death was decreed by God so that every believer could receive a body which will be free from those impediments and weaknesses resulting from the first sin of Adam and from personal sin. Physical death was not decreed as punishment for the imputed sin of Adam, but physical death was decreed to provide the occasion for the redemption of the physical body. (Romans 8:23 and 1 Corinthians 15:36)

And it should also be noted that it was not the means whereby physical death occurs, but it was the termination of physical life, which was decreed by God. And again, it is worth noting that, although neither Enoch nor Elijah slept the sleep of death, yet their physical lives were terminated. (Genesis 5:24 and 2 Kings 2:11) And likewise the physical lives of those "which are alive and remain unto the coming of the Lord" (1 Thessalonians 4:15) will also be terminated. But their physical lives will not terminate in the sleep of death. (1 Corinthians 15:51) And although the sin of Adam is imputed to every descendent of Adam, yet physical death is not caused by the imputed sin of Adam.

But rather, physical death as described in Genesis 3:19 and Ecclesiastics 12:7 is part of the remedy for the consequences of the first sin of Adam. The imputed sin of Adam renders the physical body imperfect and consequently unfit for the perfect environment of heaven. Thus "flesh and blood cannot inherit the kingdom of God." (1 Corinthians 15:50) So the physical body is discarded in accordance with Genesis 3:19, "Dust thou art, and unto dust shalt thou return.". And on the resurrection day a spiritual body will replace the physical body of each of the resurrected dead and of each of those who "are alive and remain." (1 Thessalonians 4:17) For "flesh and blood cannot inherit the kingdom of God." But while the physical lives of those who "are alive and remain" will be terminated in accordance with Ecclesiastics 12:7, yet they will not sleep the sleep of death, as noted in 1 Corinthians 15:51. And God's remedy for the consequences of the imputed sin of Adam is summarized in 1 Corinthians 15:44, "It is sown a natural body, it is raised a spiritual body."

And from the example of John the Baptist, given above, it can be seen that the imputed sin of Adam does not cause spiritual death. To further emphasize this view, what is recorded in the scriptures about Samson may be considered "— for the child shall be a Nazarite to God from the womb to the day of his death." (Judges 13:7) Among the rules prescribed for a Nazarite, it is stated in Numbers 6:8 that "All the days of his separation he is holy unto the Lord." And even though the sin of Adam most certainly was imputed to Samson, yet the scriptures clearly show that Samson was separated unto the Lord from the day of his birth until the day of his death. The foregoing observations may be stated briefly as follows:

    1.   The first sin of Adam and Eve adversely affected the entire physical creation which included the physical bodies of Adam and Eve.

    2.   The first sin of Adam and Eve resulted immediately in spiritual death.

    3.   God restored spiritual life to Adam and Eve, confirmed by coats of skins.

    4.   God decreed the termination of physical life to provide the occasion when the mortal bodies of Adam and Eve would be changed to spiritual bodies in the resurrection.

    5.   God now imputes the first sin of Adam to all descendants of Adam "that He might have mercy upon all" (Romans 11:32), and decress the termination of their physical lives so that their mortal bodies will be changed to spiritual bodies in the resurrection.

    6.   God also imputes the righteousness of Christ to every descendant of Adam at the moment of conception thus preventing any adverse spiritual consequences from the imputed sin of Adam.

VIII. THE POSSIBILITY OF REMAINING SPIRITUALLY ALIVE FROM CONCEPTION UNTIL PHYSICAL DEATH

It was shown previously that all of the descendants of Adam are spiritually alive beginning at the moment of conception. And since the only cause of spiritual death is the rejection of "the commandment" (Romans 7:9) to repent and believe, then it must follow that all of the descendants of Adam remain spiritually alive until they become aware of the command to repent and believe.

And then, if they obey that commandment to repent and believe, they continue to remain spiritually alive just as Paul would have continued to remain spiritually alive if he had obeyed "the commandment" when it came.

And if any descendant of Adam does not obey "the commandment" to repent and believe, that person dies spiritually just as Paul died spiritually.

(Romans 7:9) But as noted above, it is not necessary to die spiritually. A person may continue to be spiritually alive from the moment of conception until the termination of physical life, and further scriptural support for this view can be supplied by investigating some objections which may arise.

A better foundation for investigating these objections may be provided if we first consider the meaning of three closely related verses of scripture. These verses of scripture are: Ephesians 2:1, Ephesians 2:5 and Colossians 2:13. Each of these verses refers to every believer as being "dead in sins" previous to the time when he repented and believed the gospel. The meaning of the phrase "dead in sins" is of vital importance. The common assumption that original sin is the cause of spiritual death has made it easy to conclude that "dead in sins" simply refers to a state of spiritual death wherein every descendant of Adam is born. Since it was shown previously that original sin is not the cause of spiritual death, and that every descendant of Adam is spiritually alive when he is born into this earthly life, then it is obviously necessary to reconsider the meaning of the phrase "dead in sins".

An analysis of the phrase "dead in sins" can be accomplished by following a procedure similar to that which Paul used in the 5th chapter of Romans to show that physical death proves that the sin of Adam is imputed to all the descendants of Adam. To make this conclusion indisputable, Paul limits his observation to the span of time from Adam to Moses. For during that span of time there were no commandments of God in force except the commandment forbidding Adam and Eve to eat of the fruit of the tree of the knowledge of good and evil. And that commandment could not again be broken since it was impossible for man to enter the garden of Eden after Adam and Eve were driven out.

Then, since "sin is not imputed when there is no law" (or commandment) (Romans 5:13), the only sin, which could be imputed during the span of time from Adam to Moses, was the sin which Adam and Eve committed while they were still in the garden of Eden. And, that the first sin of Adam was indeed imputed to every descendant of Adam is evident since death entered by sin, and "death passed upon all men". (Romans 5:12) And this conclusion was reached by considering some conditions existing in the limited span of time from Adam to Moses. (Romans 5:14)

By proceeding in a similar manner, it can be shown that the phrase "dead in sins" (Ephesians 2:1&5 and Colossians 2:13) describes a spiritual condition which is entirely different from "spiritually dead".

It was previously shown that, beginning at the moment of conception, every descendant of Adam is spiritually alive. And it was also shown that the only cause of spiritual death is rejection of the command to repent and believe the gospel. (Mark 1:15) And it is impossible for a descendant of Adam to obey or to reject that commandment until he becomes aware of that commandment. Thus he remains spiritually alive until he becomes aware of that commandment, just as Paul was spiritually alive until "the commandment" came to him. (Romans 7:9)

When the commandment to repent and believe the gospel comes to any descendant of Adam, that descendant of Adam must either obey the commandment or reject the commandment. If he obeys the commandment to repent and believe the gospel, he is then a believer. But up to the time when he becomes aware of the commandment, he is described as being "dead in sins". (Ephesians 2:1&5 and Colossians 2:13)

And just as any person who obeys the commandment is described as being "dead in sins" when the commandment comes, likewise all descendants of Adam are described as being "dead in sins" when the commandment comes. But as shown previously, every person is spiritually alive until he becomes aware of the command to repent and believe the gospel. Therefor "dead in sins" as used in Ephesians 2:1&5 and Colossians 2:13 cannot mean "spiritually dead". For all persons are spiritually alive until they become aware of the command to repent and believe the gospel, and during that same period of time they are described as being "dead in sins".

What then is the meaning of the phrase "dead in sins"? To answer this question, it is necessary first to consider what death is. In the miracles of raising from the dead the daughter of Jairus (Matthew 9:18-26, Mark 5:22-43, Luke 8:41-56) and the raising from the dead of Lazarus (John 11:1-46) Jesus refers to death as sleep. In both death and sleep there is the absence of physical consciousness. Just as one who is asleep is unconscious, so also, one who is dead is unconscious. Thus one who is "dead in sins" is unconscious in sins. And it is from this state of unconsciousness that the Holy Spirit awakens a person.

And before the person is awakened by the Holy Spirit, he is spiritually alive just as the apostle Paul said in Romans 7:9 that he was spiritually alive before "the commandment came". Likewise every person is spiritually alive from the moment of conception up until the time when the Holy Spirit awakens him from that state of unconsciousness wherein he is described as being "dead in sins". The phrase "dead in sins" refers to the time in every person's life previous to the time when the Holy Spirit awakens him. And again, as noted previously, the phrase "dead in sins" does not mean "spiritually dead". But rather, the phrase, "dead in sins", refers to a state in which a person is spiritually alive but unconscious of his sins.

There are, quite naturally, many objections which may be raised to the idea that it is possible for a descendant of Adam to continue spiritually alive from the time of conception until physical death occurs. The first objection is that every descendant of Adam is spiritually dead when he is born physically. Since it was shown previously that every descendant of Adam is spiritually alive beginning at the moment of conception, this objection is therefor not valid.

A second objection is based on the language of John 3:3 where Jesus said: "Except a man be born again, he cannot see the kingdom of God". In this passage of scripture the Greek word "anothen" is translated to mean "again". But "anothen" means "from above". Now, it is obvious that if a man must be born again, it is because he is spiritually dead. But if the text is translated properly, it will read: "Except a man be born from above, he cannot see the kingdom of God.". The requirement of this text then is met at the moment of conception when (as was previously shown) the righteousness of Christ is imputed. It is at that moment that the person is born from above, and spiritual life begins. And the person remains spiritually alive until he is made aware of "the commandment" (Romans 7:9) to repent and believe. And he continues to remain spiritually alive if he obeys that commandment.

A third objection may then be raised, namely, that, if a person is spiritually alive when born, there should be no necessity to repent and believe. To answer this objection we may note, first, that, as previously stated, every person is spiritually alive when born, but is unconscious of his sins and lack of faith until he is awakened by the Holy Spirit. Thus, although every descendant of Adam is spiritually alive when he is born into this earthly life, yet he is not aware that he does not trust in Christ. It is therefor necessary for him, when "the commandment" (Romans 7:9) comes, to repent of his lack of belief and to believe or trust in the righteousness of Christ as the remedy for his personal sin and unbelief. Thus the third objection (If a person is spiritually alive when born, there should be no necessity to repent and believe.) is not valid.

A fourth objection which may be raised is that, a person is not spiritually alive until he is converted, so he could not continue to be spiritually alive from the moment of conception until the end of this earthly life. This objection may be answered by noting that spiritual life begins when the righteousness of Christ is imputed as the remedy for sin. And it was shown previously that the righteousness of Christ is imputed at the moment of conception as the remedy for the imputed sin of Adam. Thus life in Christ begins at the moment of conception, and, beginning at that moment, the person is spiritually alive. And thus it is possible for the person to continue to be spiritually alive until the end of this earthly life provided that he obeys "the commandment" (to repent and believe) when it comes. Thus the fourth objection is not valid.

Or again some may object that, since little children do not fully understand the command to repent and believe, they therefor do not qualify to possess the Spirit of Christ and consequently are not spiritually alive. In answer to this objection it may be noted that a full understanding of any particular portion of scripture is not possible for anyone, for again and again we are told that His ways are "past finding out." (Romans 11:33, Isaiah 40:28, Ecclesiastics 11:5) If a full understanding of any portion of scripture were required as the qualification for possessing the Spirit of Christ, then no one would qualify. But to answer the objection more specifically, we may note the words of Jesus in Mark 10:14 where He declares that "of such is the kingdom of God". And in Matthew 18:3 we read: "Except ye be converted, and become as little children, ye shall not enter into the kingdom of heaven." Little children are a part of His kingdom. They belong to Christ, for the righteousness of Christ is imputed to them as the remedy for the imputed sin of Adam at the moment of conception. And since they belong to Christ, it follows from Romans 8:9 that they do possess the Spirit of Christ, and thus they are spiritually alive. And further, it is humbling but yet comforting to observe that God, by His sovereign decree, chose to establish little children as the standard by which entrance into the kingdom of heaven will be determined.

To state that God creates souls which are spiritually dead, sets forth an untenable theological position. For again and again, as noted above, the scripture assures us that all children are born spiritually alive. Such was the conclusion of the Psalmist, David, when reflecting upon the death of the child born as a result of his adulterous relation with Bathsheba. The prophet Nathan was sent by the Lord to point out David's sin, and then David was assured by Nathan that "the Lord also hath put away thy sin.". (2 Samuel 12:13) Thus David was reassured that his eternal destination would still be to "dwell in the house of the Lord forever.". (Psalm 23:6) And that he knew that his child had preceded him to that same destination is shown by David's statement in 2 Samuel 12:23 "— I shall go to him, but he shall not return to me.".

One further objection, which may be raised to the idea that a state of spiritual death does not necessarily precede conversion, is based on the language of 1 John 3:14 which is translated to read: "We know that we have passed from death unto life, because we love the brethren." In this passage, as also in John 5:24, the Greek work "metabaino" is translated to mean "passed". But "metabaino" in both of these texts means "to go up over" or "to transcend". Thus the text should read: "We know that we have transcended death unto life, because we love the brethren.". Thus by transcending spiritual death by obeying the command to repent and believe, a person may continue to be spiritually alive from the moment of conception until the termination of physical life. It does appear probable, however, that the majority fall in the same category as Paul who said: "For I was alive without the law once: but when the commandment came, sin revived, and I died." (Romans 7:9) But when he became transformed on the Damascus road, Saul of Tarsus did pass "from death", and transcended death to a higher plane: everlasting life.

Some questions will arise concerning those scriptures which present a preview of the eternal consequences of sin. The description given in Matthew 25:41-46 of the dismal future awaiting the unregenerate soul must be accepted as an accurate preview of what would certainly have happened to every descendant of Adam if Christ had not died on the cross as the atonement for the sins of the world. But to assume that this preview of the judgment must take place, it must also be assumed that God was unable to accomplish the purpose for which He gave His Son. But the scripture tells us that it is God's will to "have all men to be saved." (1 Timothy 2:4) And while this may appear impossible, yet Jesus said, "with God all things are possible." (Mark 10:27) And again, Jesus said, "And I, if I be lifted up from the earth, will draw all men unto Me." (John 12:32) Thus it is obvious that the description of the judgment day given in Matthew 25:41-46 was not intended as prophecy. But rather, Matthew 25:41-46, by describing what would have been the final destination of every unregenerate soul, serves to emphasize and to magnify to its true proportion what Jesus accomplished on the cross. For the question of the eternal destiny of every descendant of Adam was decided at the cross.

It has been the tendency of orthodox interpretation of the scriptures to accept as relative those promises whereby God decrees eternal life for every descendant of Adam while accepting as absolute the threatenings of God to deliver to everlasting fire a part of the race which God created in His own image.

Such a standard of interpretation not only questions the character of God but also creates an untenable theological position which serves to diminish the spirit of unity among true believers. The solution is not in reassessing the words of the Saviour but in arranging in perspective the statements of the Lord which pertain to man's eternal destiny so that the promises of God receive priority over the threatenings of God. "For all the promises of God in Him are yea, and in Him Amen." (2 Corinthians 1:20)

And further, since the requirements of the justice of God were satisfied by the atoning death of Christ upon the cross, it is not necessary for the threatenings of God to be carried out. However, the threatenings of God continue to serve to show the believer the eternal destiny from which God saved him and thus serve further to provide the believer with an undeniable reason to be forever grateful.

The foregoing paragraphs illustrate the nature of the answers which the Scriptures provide to objections to the idea that it is possible for a person to remain spiritually alive from the moment of conception until the termination of physical life. And although objections may be multiplied and answered, truth is not finally established by answering all of the objections which may be raised. For it is not reasonable to suppose that a point could ever be reached where no further objections to truth will be raised. For while there may be an end to honest objections, yet as long as the hosts of Satan are free to go forth to deceive, for just that long, objections to truth will continue to be raised. It is not in answering objections that truth is finally confirmed. But rather, the validity of any truth is confirmed by the foundation upon which it rests. And when any truth has for its foundation any of God's sovereign decrees as set forth in the Holy Scriptures, we may safely conclude that all objections to that truth are of no merit.

And the possibility that a person may continue to remain spiritually alive from conception to the termination of physical life serves to further emphasize that the imputed sin of Adam is not the cause of spiritual death, but rather, the cause is the refusal to repent and believe the gospel. For God by His sovereign decree has stated that "the son shall not bear the iniquity of the father". (Ezekiel 18:20) And thus the descendants of Adam do not die spiritually for Adam's sin. And in similar manner it is established that God's sovereign grace is available to all. For, since God by His sovereign decree imputed the righteousness of Christ to all (Romans 5:18), thus by His own act God demonstrated, more emphatically than words can declare, that His sovereign grace is for all and available to all.

For again, since God by His sovereign decree imputed the righteousness of Christ to all, it follows then, that every descendant of Adam is spiritually alive when he begins this earthly life. And thus every descendant of Adam receives God's sovereign grace as the remedy for the imputed sin of Adam at the moment of conception. Few things provide greater assurance that God's sovereign grace is available to all than to know that every descendant of Adam receives that sovereign grace at the very beginning of this earthly life.

Thus every descendant of Adam who repents and believes the gospel may rejoice in the words of John Newton's great hymn:

Twas grace that taught my heart to fear
And grace my fears relieved.
How precious did that grace appear
The hour I first believed.

And we may rejoice further that original sin is not the cause of spiritual death. For, were that the case, then we could have no certain hope for the eternal destiny of little children whom death has taken from among us. But the same merciful God who has created all children has assured us in His word "That in heaven their angels do always behold the face of my Father which is in heaven.". (Matthew 18:10)

In brief summary, every descendant of Adam is, by God's sovereign decree, born from above at the moment of conception, and thus he enters this life spiritually alive. And he may continue to be spiritually alive until the termination of his earthly life if he obeys the commandment to repent and believe when he becomes aware of that commandment. Or if he chooses to reject that commandment, he dies spiritually just as the apostle Paul died spiritually. (See Romans 5:12-18 and 7:9 also John 3:3-7 and Ezekiel 18:4&20.)

The commandment to repent and believe comes to all. (See Luke 13:3&5 and Acts 17:30, also John 3:18 and Mark 1:15.) And when they respond to the call of God, they then begin to trust in Christ. Thus they transcend spiritual death and experience the peace that passes all understanding. (Philippians 4:7) (John 5:24) But the descendant of Adam who has rejected the commandment and died spiritually is still faced with the requirement to repent and believe. And the fact that the righteousness of Christ was imputed to him at the moment of conception is his assurance that God has provided for him (as well as for all the other descendants of Adam) a place among the elect. But to occupy that place among the elect, he must repent and believe.

But let us remember that repenting and believing does not save us. It is God who saves us by His grace according to Ephesians 2:8. The requirement to repent and believe is God's requirement given by Jesus Christ in Mark 1:15. And there is no other way to God, for Jesus said in Luke 13:3,5 "— Except ye repent, ye shall all likewise perish.". And again in John 3:18 Jesus said: "— he that believeth not is condemned already—". But to those who come to Him in response to His command to repent and believe the gospel, He gives this promise: "— him that cometh to me I will in no wise cast out.". (John 6:37). And thus God's sovereign grace is available to all.

IX. GOD'S ALL - INCLUSIVE SALVATION

In the preceding pages it has been shown that original sin does not determine the eternal destiny of any descendant of Adam and Eve. It has also been shown that God's sovereign grace is available to every person. It is then reasonable to ask whether every person will repent and believe the gospel and receive God's sovereign grace and be saved.

To answer this question, it is logical to ask whether God can save everyone. In Matthew 19:26 Jesus gave the answer: "with God all things are possible". Then since God can save everyone, the final question is: Will God save everyone?.

To answer this question, it should be determined whether there is any reason why God should save everyone. And of all the reasons that could be given, the fact that "God created man in His own image" (Genesis 1:27), is among the best. But God's justice demands a penalty for man's sin. God threatens hell fire to all who refuse to repent. But God's love for the souls of men forbids Him to deliver the sinner to hell fire. And so before God created man, God drew the plan of salvation so that the demands of His justice would be satisfied by the atoning death of Christ upon the cross. Then with the demands of His justice satisfied, God is free to use whatever means His love ordains to compel every sinner to repent and believe the gospel. God's justice cannot ever satisfy the demands of God's love. But God's love did satisfy the demands of God's justice at the cross.

Thus God is at liberty to save everyone. Yet all of the best reasons which may be given why God should save everyone are not sufficient to assure that God will save everyone. It is only God Himself who can give the assurance that He will save everyone. And God does give that assurance by stating what His will is and then by declaring that He will accomplish His will. God states that He "will have all men to be saved, and to come unto the knowledge of the truth.". (1 Timothy 2:4) God further declares what His will is in 2 Peter 3:9 when He states that He is "not willing that any should perish, but that all should come to repentance.". And then God dispels every doubt that He will accomplish His will by stating that He "worketh all things after the counsel of His own will.". (Ephesians 1:11)

Further confirmation that God will save everyone is provided by the words of Jesus in John 12:32, "And I, if I be lifted up from the earth, will draw all men unto Me." This can hardly mean that Jesus will attract men unto Himself. For Isaiah 53:2&3 says "— He hath no form nor comeliness; and when we shall see Him, there is no beauty that we should desire Him. He is despised and rejected of men; a man of sorrows, and acquainted with grief; and we hid as it were our faces from Him; He was despised, and we esteemed Him not."

The fact that God gave His only begotten Son (John 3:16) shows that God will stop at nothing to save sinners. God's love for the souls of sinners is infinite. Consequently the demands of the love of God can never be satisfied with anything less than the salvation of every soul.

The justice of God demands a penalty for every sin committed by anyone who is aware of God's requirement. However, the demands of the eternal justice of God were satisfied on the cross by "the Lamb of God which taketh away the sin of the world.". (John 1:29) The love of God satisfied the demands of the eternal justice of God, but the eternal justice of God cannot ever satisfy the demands of the love of God. If the eternal justice of God could send a sinner to hell, this would not satisfy the demands of the love of God.

The love of God can be satisfied when God compels every sinner to repent and believe the gospel. Acts 9:3-6 tells how God compelled Saul of Tarsus to repent and believe the gospel. And thus God demonstrates that He does not leave to the sinner the choice whether or not to repent and believe the gospel. And further, God declares that He does not leave the choice to the sinner, for Jesus said: "Ye have not chosen Me, but I have chosen you.". (John 15:16)

The manner in which Christ draws men unto Himself is suggested in the following lines of a hymn by Isaac Watts:

> *How sweet and awful is the place,*
> *With Christ within the doors,*
> *While everlasting love displays*
> *The choicest of her stores.*
>
> *Twas the same love that spread the feast*
> *That sweetly forced us in;*
> *Else we had still refused to taste,*
> *And perished in our sin.*

In this hymn Isaac Watts comprehended well the truth that is recorded in Isaiah 6 and is referred to by Paul when presenting the gospel to the Jews at Rome: "Well spake the Holy Ghost by Esaias the prophet unto our fathers, saying, Go unto this people, and say, Hearing ye shall hear, and shall not understand; and seeing ye shall see, and not perceive: For the heart of this people is waxed gross, and their ears are dull of hearing, and their eyes have they closed; lest they should see with their eyes, and hear with their ears, and understand with their heart, and should be converted, and I should heal them." (Acts 28:25-27) Man is often unwilling to be converted. But what Isaac Watts apparently did not comprehend was that, since God compels some to repent and believe the gospel, then it must follow that God will compel every sinner to repent and believe the gospel. For "God is no respecter of persons." (Acts 10:34)

For additional confirmation that God will save every soul, Romans 11:26 may be considered. It is obvious from the context that Paul is not referring to the spiritual "children of Abraham" (Galatians 3:7) when he says, "All Israel shall be saved.". Then again, since "all Israel shall be saved" (Romans 11:26), and since "there is no difference between the Jew and the Greek" (Romans 10:12), then God will save every soul. It should be noted that all are invited to come to Christ to be saved, but they do not come until they are compelled to come. This is illustrated in the parable of Luke 14:16-24. And it should be recognized that a parable is for the purpose of illustration and not for establishing doctrine. This parable illustrates that God does compel man to respond to an invitation. Man is either brought by God as in the case of the mentally impaired, or else under normal circumstances God compels man to come to Him to be saved. This parable illustrates that more than a simple invitation is required to bring men to Christ. They must be either brought or else compelled to come. "We are labourers together with God" (1 Corinthians 3:9) to compel men to come while God also compels them to come. Jesus said, "No man can come to Me, except the Father which hath sent Me draw him." (John 6:44) The urgency of the gospel is not that man may forfeit his salvation by delaying his acceptance of God's gift of eternal life, but rather that, the longer man delays, the longer he will forfeit the benefits of the gospel, and the more he will diminish his opportunity to lay up treasures in heaven, for "the night cometh, when no man can work". (John 9:4) Men come to Christ because they are compelled to come. Some are compelled by love, some by reason, some by fear, some by loneliness, some by suffering, some by unusual events or circumstances. But when Christ draws them, they are compelled to come unto Him.

Christ compelled Saul of Tarsus to come unto Him on the Damascus road. (Acts 9:1-20) It can be said with confidence that Christ does draw all men unto Himself, for this is what He said that He would do. Christ draws all men unto Himself by whatever means He chooses. And He draws all men unto Himself by compelling power.

Christ promises to draw all men unto Himself. And the promises of God always take precedence over the threatenings of God. For God gave His Son as a sacrifice upon the cross to insure that the promise of Christ to draw all men unto Himself would be fulfilled. But God made no sacrifice to insure that His threatenings would be carried out. Rather, the sacrifice of Christ upon the cross was made to insure that the threatenings of God would not be carried out.

And nothing can prevent God from accomplishing His will to "have all men to be saved, and to come unto the knowledge of the truth". (1 Timothy 2:4) The demands of God's justice were satisfied by the sacrifice of Christ upon the cross. Then to satisfy the demands of His love, God established grace as the means whereby sinners may receive the benefits of the atoning sacrifice of Christ upon the cross. Hence to accomplish His will to save every soul, it is necessary for God only to compel every sinner to repent and believe the gospel.

And God then leaves us a further word of assurance when we read in Philippians 1:6 "— Being confident of this very thing, that He which hath begun a good work in you will perform it until the day of Jesus Christ.". That "good work" is begun in every descendant of Adam at the moment of conception when God imputes the righteousness of Christ as the remedy for the imputed sin of Adam. And that "good work" is continued at the time of conversion when the person becomes a believer.

And just as He compelled the spiritually dead Saul of Tarsus to repent and believe the gospel on the Damascus road, God will also compel every descendant of Adam to repent and believe the gospel. For "God is no respecter of persons." (Acts 10:34)

God will accomplish His will to "have all men to be saved, and to come unto the knowledge of the truth". (1 Timothy 2:4) And God then will be glorified. And it will be then that every knee will bow and every tongue will confess "that Jesus Christ is Lord to the glory of God the Father". (Philippians 2:11)

So thus it will be that the Lord Almighty will be true to His word without carrying out His threat of hell fire for the sinner. Since "God so loved the world that He gave His only begotten Son" (John 3:16), it is clear that the love of God provided the way to satisfy the demands of the eternal justice of God. The love of God is therefor not restricted by the justice of God. It is obvious then that the love of God will determine how God will accomplish His will to "have all men to be saved, and to come unto the knowledge of the truth". (1 Timothy 2:4)

In conclusion, it is certain that God's sovereign grace will accomplish God's sovereign will by saving every soul. God cannot and will not be defeated. God would not be sovereign if anyone could prevent Him from accomplishing His will. From Genesis to Revelation the Bible confirms the sovereignty of God. When God created man, He did not create him with the ability to annul God's sovereignty. Because He is sovereign, God can accomplish His will "that all should come to repentance." (2 Peter 3:9) It is God's will that all men "be saved" (1 Timothy 2:4), and Christ confirmed that He would accomplish His will when He said "And I, if I be lifted up from the earth, will draw all men unto Me." (John 12:32)

The foregoing conclusions may call into question some doctrinal positions of long standing as well as some practices which have been often accepted as valid expressions of New Testament standards. Nevertheless those positions and practices, which have served only to fetter the church, must be either altered or discarded to accommodate the pure word of God, the Bible. It will obviously be the reader's prerogative and duty to determine how accurately the foregoing conclusions have reflected the total scope of the Bible. And it hardly needs to be said that to accept the false for the sake of novelty or to reject the true to sustain and perpetuate the fond errors of the past will in either case evoke the displeasure of our sovereign God.

Let every reader then make diligent search, with all readiness of mind, to see whether these things are so, as did those noble Bereans to whom Luke refers in Acts 17:10&11. And let us all resolve to pursue with vigor the path where God's truth leads us.

Because of the limitation of space and the urgency of time, the foregoing observations will of necessity leave many questions unanswered. But these observations have not been presented as an answer to questions as much as, hopefully, to give a more scriptural reflection of the true character of God. And so with this apology, the efforts expended in presenting the preceding pages are dedicated to the memory of my son, Timothy Earl Bower. And because my memories of Timothy have served to inspire and motivate me to include the most vital, as well as the most essential, portions of this manuscript, it is appropriate that these lines should be concluded with the tribute which I had previously written:

IN MEMORY
OF
TIMOTHY EARL BOWER

Timothy was born February 18, 1962 and died July 25, 1986 at the age of 24 years. Timothy is my boy. I did not say that Timothy was my boy, but I said rather, that Timothy is my boy. For because God is stronger than Satan, Timothy now lives in a better land. And they call that land Heaven.

Timothy lived in a world that is cruel and taught him some things which are not ordained of God. "But where sin abounded, grace did much more abound." (Romans 5:20) And God "who worketh all things after the counsel of His own will" (Ephesians 1:11) created Timothy for the same final end for which He creates all mortals. The central message of the Holy Scriptures is that, above all else, God's will is to save every descendant of Adam. So great was God's desire to accomplish man's salvation that He sent His Son, Jesus, to die for the sins of man. The eternal salvation of every person has always been the highest priority of God's will. And Christ's death upon the cross is God's highest expression of His will to save every person.

And since He is omnipotent, God is always able to accomplish His will. And since God "worketh all things after the counsel of His own will," (Ephesians 1:11) it is impossible for even one soul to be lost eternally. For God "will have all men to be saved, and to come unto the knowledge of the truth." (I Timothy 2:4) God cannot fail to accomplish His will, and thus every soul will be saved. But to receive assurance of our salvation now, we must obey the command of Jesus, "Repent ye, and believe the gospel." (Mark 1:15) Timothy repented and believed the gospel.

The gentle breeze blows across Timothy's grave on a hillside in New Alexandria, Pennsylvania. But Timothy is not there. Timothy is in Heaven. In my human frailty I would call Timothy back again, for I loved him very much. But God has abundantly compensated me for my loss of Timothy. For when Timothy died, a decree was issued from the throne of God stating that the community of Eternity was to be revised. And so they extended the boundary of that part of Eternity called Heaven. And they extended the boundary of Heaven to the boundary of my earthly habitation. And so now Timothy lives right next door.

So until that day when God extends the boundary of Heaven again to erase the boundary of my earthly home, I wait with great anticipation to embrace my boy, Timothy, and to fulfill some cherished dreams with him and to share with him God's promised joy. "The Lord gave, and the Lord hath taken away; blessed be the name of the Lord." (Job 1:21)

David E. Bower

And finally, lest any reader should wrongly suppose that God has spoken to me in the same manner as He spoke to the prophets and the apostles, it should be noted that the decree, issued from the throne of God when Timothy died, is the same decree that is issued from the throne of God when the spirit of each descendant of Adam "shall return unto God who gave it.". (Ecclesiastics 12:7) And that decree refers to the place described by the promise of Jesus in John 14:2, "I go to prepare a place for you.". And that this promise applies to every descendant of Adam is confirmed by the promise of Jesus: "And I, if I be lifted up from the earth, will draw all men unto Me.". (John 12:32) It is my hope that it will be evident that God has spoken to me through His word, so the following observations are included.

The first chapter of Genesis gives the framework of the decrees by which the Lord progressively accomplished the creation of the heaven and the earth and all things therein. However it is well to note that, although the first chapter of Genesis does not refer to it, the physical creation was accomplished by an almost infinite number of decrees which insured that even the most minute detail would be according to God's plan. Every detail of the physical creation was accomplished by a specific decree of the Lord as noted in John 1:3 "All things were made by Him; —". That God decrees even the most minute details is attested to by Jesus in Matthew 10:30. And knowing that God is concerned about every detail of the physical creation, it can be safely concluded that God is even more concerned about every detail of the new creation in which sinners are made new creatures in Christ.

The first chapter of Genesis shows that God's decrees, by which He accomplished the physical creation, follow a logical, progressive sequence. And the four gospels also show that God's decrees by which He accomplished every detail of the new creation also follow a logical progressive sequence, for example: the birth, the earthly ministry, the crucifixion, the burial, and the resurrection of Christ. Thus it is established that God accomplishes all that He does by His own decrees.

Therefor it is scripturally justifiable to say that a decree is issued from the throne of God every time a soul departs this earthly life. For when a soul enters the presence of the Lord, it is an occasion of the most enormous magnitude, because God gave His Son to make certain that this occasion would occur. And fitting to the greatness of the occasion, it is appropriate that the decree issued from the throne of God at that time should specify that the community of Eternity should be revised, for God is never too early, and God is never too late. It is sometimes mistakenly assumed that the final home of the redeemed was prepared at the time when the world was created. For in that scene from the 25th chapter of Matthew the King says to those on

His right hand "— inherit the kingdom prepared for you from the foundation of the world". (Matthew 25:34) But since Jesus said, "I go to prepare a place for you." (John 14:2), it is obvious that He had not previously done so. This eliminates the possibility that the eternal home of the redeemed was prepared as a part of the physical creation. And since God is never too early and never too late, it is reasonable to say that Jesus prepares a place for each soul when that soul departs this earthly life, and thus, by a decree from the throne of God, the community of Eternity is revised. And as it is for every soul, so it was for my son, Timothy. The boundary, which I must cross to enter heaven, once seemed far away. But when Timothy died, he entered Heaven, and the boundary of Heaven seemed then to be right next door. And the words of the second verse of the song "Beulah Land" by Edgar Page provide a fitting conclusion to these comments:

My Savior comes and walks with me,
And sweet communion here have we;
He gently leads me by His hand,
For this is Heaven's border land.

APPENDIX A

It should be noted, when considering the effects of original sin, that the imperfections of nature cannot with absolute certainty be attributed to the effects of original sin. The difficulties encountered in either supporting or refuting the conclusion, that all imperfections of nature are the consequence of original sin, can be illustrated by considering the topic of the "morning stars" of Job 38:7. And it should be noted that the holy scriptures alone provide the only sure foundation upon which sound theological conclusions can be established. And when the holy scriptures do not provide a clear answer to any question, then the end product of all human effort to provide an answer to that question must be labelled speculation. And for those answers which elude the inquiring mind, we must wait until that day when, as the apostle Paul suggests in 1 Corinthians 13:12, we shall know as we also are known.

The topic of the "morning stars" of Job 38:7 illustrates the complexity and the futility of attempting to determine the total effects of original sin and the imputed sin of Adam. There are at least two possible meanings of "morning stars" which can be derived without doing violence to the text. The first is that "morning stars" refers to a certain group of stars which were included in the inanimate part of the original creation. The second meaning of "morning stars" is taken to be "angels". But it must be noted that, if any absolutely conclusive evidence exists for determining the meaning of "morning stars", that evidence is elusive.

That the "morning stars" of Job 38:7 were a certain group of stars of the original creation is suggested by man's investigations of the inanimate part of creation. By means of very sensitive listening equipment, it has been possible to hear the sound waves which are emitted by inanimate material such as wood or steel or stone. The sound waves emitted from inanimate material do not have a musical quality. But it is possible that in the original creation the sound waves emitted did have a musical quality, and thus it is possible that the "morning stars" did emit sound waves with a musical quality. The fact that inanimate material does not now produce sound waves having a musical quality does not eliminate the possibility that in the original creation it may have been so.

For it is conceivable that the original creation did suffer from some cataclysmic event sometime in the past so that the condition described in Romans 8:22 now prevails throughout all creation, and thus the inanimate part of creation is no longer capable of emitting sound waves having a musical quality. Whether the condition which causes the whole creation to groan and travail in pain (Romans 8:22) can be attributed to the effects of the fall of Satan (Revelation 12:4) or to the effects of the original sin of Adam (Genesis 3:6) is not certain. For the fact that "all the sons of God shouted for joy" suggests the possibility that the "morning stars sang together" at some time previous to the fall of Satan.

But it is reasonable to allow that the sound waves emitted by the inanimate part of the original creation could have harmonized to produce a quality of music superior to the best quality of music produced by the efforts of mortal man. But it should be noted that, since then, man has under divine inspiration produced a quality of music which, according to scriptural standards, is acceptable for use in the worship of God. Hence it seems reasonable to allow that the "morning stars" of the inanimate part of the original creation could also have produced a musical harmony acceptable for use in the worship of God. And since music is established by the scriptures as an important element in the worship of God, it is reasonable to suppose that God may have created the stars for the purpose, not only of illuminating the heavens, but also of providing a continuous symphony for the listening pleasure of the animate part of the original creation, and even more for the listening pleasure of God. For Revelation 4:11 says, "— for Thou hast created all things, and for thy pleasure they are and were created."

It also is necessary to consider the possibility that, since the book of Job is poetry, the words "morning stars" may be a poetic expression used to describe a group of animate beings, probably "angels". This view seems to be both supported and contradicted by the context. For the mention also in verse 7 of "the sons of God" gives rise to the thought that the general reference of this verse is to "angels", for it is reasonably certain that "the sons of God" mentioned both here and in Job 2:1 are angels. But, again, the fact that the "morning stars" are referred to separate from "the sons of God" suggests that they are not identical. And this view is further supported by the fact that their activities are not identical: the "morning stars" sang together while the "sons of God" shouted for joy. And thus it seems that the case for equating "morning stars" with "angels" is lost. However, one more possibility must be examined.

It can be reasonably deducted from the scriptures that some similarity exists in the appearance of men and angels. And it can also be reasonably deducted from the scriptures that considerable similarity exists in the appearance of Christ and men, for God created man in His own image. (Genesis 1:27) And further, Christ took upon Him the form of man. (John 1:14) Thus it is not beyond the realm of reason to allow that Christ could appear either as a man or as the angel of the Lord.

Because the visitor in Genesis 18:1-15 and Genesis 32:24-30 and Judges 6:11-22 and Judges 13:8-21 was a man and was identified as the Lord, it is obvious that the man was an angel. And also, specifically, the man was the angel of the Lord and was so identified in Judges 13:13,15,16,17,18,20&21. Thus it is obvious that the term "the angel of the Lord" refers to Deity. And because of the relation of Judges 13:18 and Isaiah 9:6 (both of which texts refer to Someone whose name is called Wonderful), it is reasonable to conclude that the Deity of the above texts of this paragraph is Christ. And it is no less certain that Christ is "the bright and morning star" of Revelation 22:16. Then, since "**THE** bright and morning star" of Revelation 22:16 is also "**THE** angel of the Lord" of Genesis 16:10 and Judges 13:18, then it is logical to allow that the "morning stars" of Job 38:7 could be some of the angels of God, some of which were seen in Genesis 28:12 and 32:1.

Based on the foregoing observations, it must be noted that absolutely conclusive evidence for determining the meaning of "morning stars" of Job 38:7 remains elusive. And although the desired goal has not been reached, it is hoped that these mental gymnastics and semantic maneuvers will be more than a source of entertainment. Again, it is hoped that the observations presented here will be useful to any who may continue the search for that evidence which will confirm the correct meaning of "morning stars" of Job 38:7. And it is hoped, above all, that these brief notes will be a source of encouragement to all who seek to confirm their relationship to Christ who is "**THE** bright and morning star" of Revelation 22:16, and who is the Creator and the Saviour of all mankind.

APPENDIX B

In the process of time the effects of original sin have become more visible and more pronounced and have multiplied and have been magnified. This process will go on, and the effects of the fall of man in the garden of Eden will reach unprecedented proportions in the seven year period of time which is referred to in the prophetic scriptures and which is commonly designated as the Great Tribulation. The effects of original sin can be seen in more complete perspective by considering some observations relative to the Great Tribulation.

The Great Tribulation is seven years of the age of grace. That the Great Tribulation is part of the age of grace is confirmed by the picture given to us in Revelation 7:9-14. That picture shows us "a great multitude, which no man could number". And verse 14 tells us that this great multitude are "they which came out of great tribulation, and have washed their robes, and made them white in the blood of the Lamb." They were saved by grace. Salvation is <u>always</u> by grace and through faith as stated in Ephesians 2:8. Jesus said, "Heaven and earth shall pass away, but my words shall not pass away." (Matthew 24:35) Salvation by grace and through faith will continue during the Great Tribulation, and thus the Great Tribulation will be part of the age of grace.

The first resurrection and the rapture will include all of that "great multitude" (Revelation 7:9) of martyrs and living saints who came out of the Great Tribulation (Revelation 7:14) For, according to 1 Corinthians 15:51&52, all saints, including those who are alive at the time of the first resurrection, will receive their resurrection bodies at the same instant. Thus it is obvious that the first resurrection and the rapture cannot precede the Great Tribulation. Otherwise the martyrs and the living "elect" (Matthew 24:22) of the Great Tribulation would not be included in the first resurrection and the rapture.

That the first resurrection and the rapture cannot precede the Great Tribulation is again confirmed in 2 Thessalonians 2:1-4. The "man of sin" referred to in 2 Thessalonians 2:3 is obviously the same person who Jesus refers to as "the abomination of desolation spoken of by Daniel the prophet." (Matthew 24:15) For Jesus refers to the time when this person (the abomination of desolation) will "stand in the holy place." Likewise 2 Thessalonians 2:4 shows the "man of sin" seated "in the temple of God, shewing himself that he is God." And Daniel 9:27 identifies this person as the one who will come to power at the midpoint of the seventieth week of the "seventy weeks of years" of Daniel 9:24. The same persons are shown engaged in the same activities during the seventieth week as in the Great Tribulation. This identifies the seventieth week as the Great Tribulation. The "abomination of desolation" (Matthew 24:15) is the beast of Revelation 13:11 who comes to power at the midpoint of the Great Tribulation after the first beast of Revelation 13:1 has continued in power for forty-two months. (Revelation 13:5)

The "abomination of desolation" (Matthew 24:15) and "the man of sin" (2 Thessalonians 2:3) and the second "beast" (Revelation 13:11) are all one and the same person. And, as noted previously, the second beast (Revelation 13:11) will take power at the midpoint of the Great Tribulation. And, according to 2 Thessalonians 2:1-3, the first resurrection and the rapture cannot take place until after the "man of sin" is revealed. Therefor the first resurrection and the rapture will take place at some time after the first three and one half years of the Great Tribulation.

It has been proposed by some that "the day of the Lord" (2 Thessalonians 2:2) means the Great Tribulation. But if we say that "the day of the Lord" means the Great Tribulation, then we arrive at a paradox. For 2 Thessalonians 2:3 states that that day will not come until "the man of sin" is revealed. And comparing Daniel 9:27 and Matthew 24:15 and 2 Thessalonians 2:3&4 and Revelation 13:5&11, it becomes obvious that the "man of sin" will not be revealed until the mid-point of the seven years of the Great Tribulation. The paradox is that if we say that "the day of the Lord" means the Great Tribulation, then the Great Tribulation will have been in progress for three and one half years before the Great Tribulation begins.

But if we follow the well established rule of interpreting scripture consistent with the context then no such paradox will exist. For the context defines "the day of the Lord" as "the coming of our Lord Jesus Christ, and our gathering together unto Him," which is nothing else than the first resurrection and the rapture. And, as previously noted, the first resurrection and the rapture will not occur until the "man of sin" is revealed. And, as previously noted, "the man of sin" will be revealed at the mid-point of the Great Tribulation. And the first resurrection and the rapture will therefor occur <u>after</u> the mid-point of the Great Tribulation.

Below is shown a pictorial representation of the order in which the scriptures show that the first resurrection and the rapture will occur relative to other events and the conditions of the Great Tribulation.

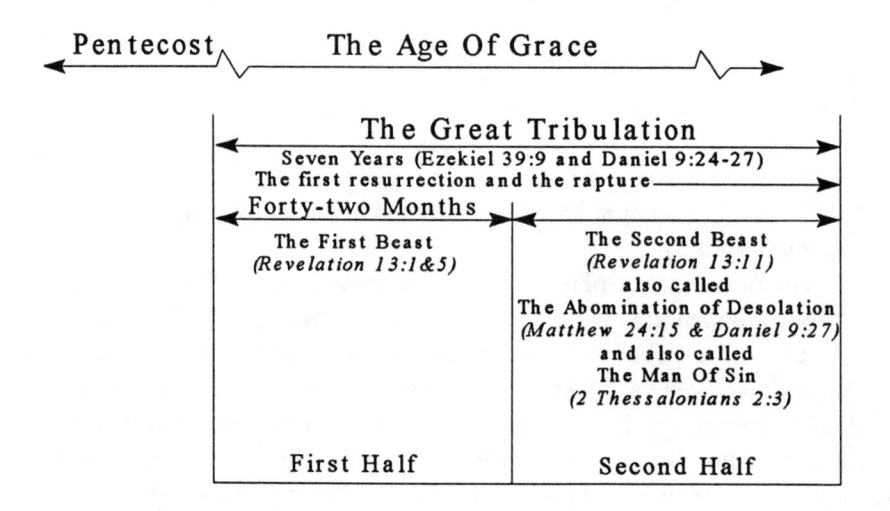

```
       Pentecost        The Age Of Grace
   <─────────────────────────────────────────>

              ┌──────────────────────────────────────────┐
              │         The Great Tribulation            │
              │  Seven Years (Ezekiel 39:9 and Daniel 9:24-27) │
              │  The first resurrection and the rapture ──>│
              │ ◄── Forty-two Months ──► │                │
              │     The First Beast      │   The Second Beast   │
              │   (Revelation 13:1&5)    │  (Revelation 13:11)  │
              │                          │     also called      │
              │                          │ The Abomination of Desolation │
              │                          │ (Matthew 24:15 & Daniel 9:27) │
              │                          │    and also called   │
              │                          │    The Man Of Sin    │
              │                          │ (2 Thessalonians 2:3)│
              │                          │                      │
              │       First Half         │     Second Half      │
              └──────────────────────────────────────────┘
```

The first resurrection and the rapture will occur sometime after the man of sin (2 Thessalonians 2:3) is revealed at the mid-point of the Great Tribulation. And from the description of the first resurrection and the rapture given in Matthew 24:29-31, and from the three descriptions given in Revelation 6:12-17 and 11:11&12 and 16:12-15, it appears certain that the first resurrection and the rapture will occur at the end of second half of the Great Tribulation.

That the first resurrection and the rapture will not precede the Great Tribulation is confirmed, as noted previously, by Paul's first letter to the Corinthians.

In 1 Corinthians 15:51&52 three notable facts are confirmed:

1. All of the redeemed will receive resurrection bodies: "we shall all be changed". (Verse 51)

2. All of the redeemed will receive their resurrection bodies in an instant: "In a moment in the twinkling of an eye". (Verse 52)

3. All of the redeemed will receive their resurrection bodies at the same instant: "at the last trump". (Verse 52)

When verse 51 says "we shall all be changed", this includes all of the redeemed, past, present, and future. The scripture will never be altered. (Matthew 24:35)

When verse 52 says "at the last trump", this eliminates the theory that the first resurrection will take place in two parts, the first part occurring before the Great Tribulation and the second part after the Great Tribulation.

Obviously the first resurrection must take place during or after the Great Tribulation to include all of those who will die for their faith during the Great Tribulation. Since 1 Thessalonians 4:16 states that "the dead in Christ shall rise first" then the first resurrection must precede the rapture. Therefor the rapture must take place after the death of the last of the martyrs of the Great Tribulation.

That the first resurrection will occur at or near the end of the Great Tribulation is further confirmed by Revelation 20:4-6. In his vision John (Revelation 1:9) sees in verse 4 of the 20th chapter, seated upon their thrones, those who are to reign with Christ for one thousand years. And John specifically mentions that, included in this group who are to reign with Christ for one thousand years, are those who are martyred for their faith during the Great Tribulation. And verses 5 and 6 show that all of this group of martyrs will have "part in the first resurrection." For no one will live and reign with Christ for the one thousand years except those who will have had part in the first resurrection and the rapture.

Also, it is important to note that when Jesus prayed in John 17:15, He specifically declined to ask the heavenly Father to take the believer out of the world. But because of the present worsening world conditions, some degree of anxiety may be present among some believers concerning the prospect of being on this earth during the Great Tribulation. However, it is not possible that conditions during the Great Tribulation will become so bad that the heavenly Father will no longer be able to answer the prayer of Jesus in John 17:15 that the Father would "keep them from the evil." God not only can, but will, answer every prayer that Jesus prayed.

There are no limits to God's ability to care for His people. But God sometimes chooses to protect and sustain His people in the presence of adverse conditions and circumstances rather than to remove His people from the presence of adversity. God chose to allow the Israelites to remain in Egypt under adverse conditions while He brought the ten plagues upon the Egyptians. (See Exodus 7:14 through Exodus 12:30) And it should be noted that, while the Egyptians suffered greatly, the Israelites, all of whom were in Egypt at that time, were spared. Likewise, when "the seven angels" (Revelation 16:1) pour out the vials of the wrath of God upon the earth, God will be able to sustain and protect His people just as He sustained and protected the Israelites from the ten plagues in Egypt. It is reasonable to conclude that the martyrs of the Great Tribulation will not be victims of the wrath of God which is poured out upon the earth during the Great Tribulation, but rather, they will be the victims of the Antichrist.

When God's wrath is poured out upon the earth during the Great Tribulation, Christians will not be the victims of God's wrath. For God assures us in His word that He has "not appointed us to wrath." (1 Thessalonians 5:9)

Again, from the book of Revelation, additional confirmation is provided which shows that the first resurrection and the rapture will occur "immediately after the tribulation of those days." (Matthew 24:29)

The central message of the book of Revelation is presented in three separate accounts which may be designated as (1) **The Seven Seals,** (2) **The Seven Trumpets,** and (3) **The Seven Last Plagues.** Each of these three accounts is divided into seven periods of time. Each of these seven periods of time presents a different aspect of the events and conditions occurring in the corresponding period of time of the other two accounts. For example, the events and conditions described under the first seal and the first trumpet and the first of the seven last plagues all occur during the same period of time.

It can be agreed that the abundance of symbolism found in the book of Revelation does provide some basis to doubt that the three accounts

(The Seven Seals, The Seven Trumpets, and The Seven Last Plagues) each cover the same seven year period of time. But an examination of the sixth seal and the sixth trumpet and the sixth of the seven last plagues confirms that the events and conditions of the sixth seal and the sixth trumpet and the sixth of the seven last plagues all occur during the same period of time. For in all three of these accounts one event is specifically mentioned, and that event is the second coming of Christ. And since the second coming can occur only once, there can be no doubt that each of the three accounts do cover the same period of time.

Under the sixth seal the second coming is mentioned (Revelation 6:12-17) similar to the description in Matthew 24:29&30. Under the sixth trumpet the first resurrection is described (Revelation 11:12) when God's two witnesses are restored to life and are called by a great voice from heaven to "Come up hither.". The first resurrection is part of the second coming. Under the sixth of the seven last plagues the second coming is referred to in Revelation 16:15 similar to the description in 1 Thessalonians 5:2. The words "Blessed is he that watcheth" confirm that Revelation 16:15 refers to the rapture. Those included in "he that watcheth" are the same ones "which are alive and remain" in 1 Thessalonians 4:17. This is the same event described by Jesus in Matthew 24:42 and Luke 12:37. The sequence of events given in the 16th chapter of Revelation indicate that this event will occur shortly before "Armageddon". (Revelation 16:16). And, as was shown previously, this event will occur only once, and that will be "at the last trump". (1 Corinthians 15:52)

One further observation relative to the Great Tribulation is found in Zechariah 14:4&5. This scripture is often viewed as a description of Jesus returning to the earth at the end of the Great Tribulation. And Matthew 24:29&30 definitely does place the return of Christ to the earth "immediately after the tribulation of those days." But, since the Great Tribulation is then ended, Zechariah 14:4&5 cannot apply to the end of the Great Tribulation because verse 5 says "ye shall flee like as ye fled from before the earthquake in the days of Uzziah king of Judah." And since the return of Christ to the earth will take place "immediately after the tribulation of those days," then there will be no reason to flee at the end of the Great Tribulation. Therefor Zechariah 14:4&5 must apply to a time prior to the end of the Great Tribulation when it will be necessary to flee.

And there will be a time during the Great Tribulation when there will be a definite and urgent reason to flee. That reason is given in Matthew 24:21 after the instructions of Jesus to "flee into the mountains." (Matthew 24:16) And the urgency of that flight "into the mountains" is comparable to the flight "before the earthquake in the days of Uzziah king of Judah." (Zechariah 14:5) The timing of that flight "into the mountains" according to Matthew 24:15 and Daniel 9:27 is at the mid-point of the Great Tribulation. And thus the obvious timing of the events of Zechariah 14:4&5 is not at the end of the Great Tribulation but rather at the mid-point of the Great Tribulation. And further, it then becomes obvious that Zechariah 14:4&5 is not a literal description of events occurring at the time of the return of Christ to the earth. But rather, this scripture is a symbolic description of assurance that God will provide some means of escape from some of the persecutions of the Great Tribulation as indicated in Daniel 11:34.

From the foregoing observations it should become obvious that scripture should always be interpreted by other scripture beginning with the context. It should also be obvious that some prophetic scriptures may not be understood until they are fulfilled.

In conclusion, it is appropriate that these observations relative to the Great tribulation should end with an observation concerning how the Great Tribulation will end. Contrary to the opinions of notable scholars, the Great Tribulation will end with the first resurrection. In the twentieth chapter of the book of Revelation, verse 4, John is given a picture or a vision of the saints of God on thrones and ready to reign with Christ for one thousand years. And included in that multitude of saints on their thrones are the martyrs of the Great Tribulation. And when John is given this picture or vision, he is also given the message from God: "This is the first resurrection." The seven years of this earth's most terrible days, known as the Great Tribulation, will end with the most glorious event in which any of the human race has ever been involved: **THE FIRST RESURRECTION**.

APPENDIX C

Among the factors which contribute to magnify the effects of original sin, none is of more far-reaching consequences than the distortion of spiritual truth. The spiritual truths of the Holy Scriptures are provided to guide mortals in those paths where the effects of original sin will have the least detrimental effects. And since the sin of Adam was imputed to every descendent of Adam, then the effects of original sin will be seen in the activities of every man.

It then becomes obvious that distortions of spiritual truth may often be found even in the best efforts of man to proclaim the gospel. Therefor the Holy Scriptures must be the standard by which distortions of spiritual truth can be detected and avoided. When distortions of spiritual truth are accepted, they often take precedence over proclaiming the gospel. Therefor it is urgently necessary that every creed and doctrine be continuously compared with the Holy Scriptures in order that the church may not be hindered in its primary task of fulfilling the Great Commission of Matthew 28:19&20.

There is a critical need among believers today for a more accurate understanding of Bible teaching about three topics, which affect the church. These three topics are:
1. The baptism of the Holy Spirit.
2 Speaking in tongues.
3. Healing.

In each of these three categories there were special events during the period of transition from Mosaic law to grace. These events are recorded in the Book of Acts. These special events illustrated for us the nature and the character of the Holy Spirit. These special events also served to help to establish the New Testament church.

When the process of transition from law to grace was complete and the New Testament church was firmly established, these special events had served their purpose. Some modification then appeared in God's program of bestowing His grace upon mortals. In place of these special events, God's ordained program for dispensing His grace was henceforth to be defined by the inspired epistles. And hence these special events could not serve as precedents for the activities of the New Testament church.

The epistles in some cases were addressed to particular individual churches and in some cases to the church in general. These epistles were God's permanent way of communicating with His church. Also these epistles contained God's permanent instructions to the church. And the fact that even the earlier epistles, although sometimes addressed to specific churches, yet applied also to the New Testament church in general, indicated that already the church was "builded together for an habitation of God through the Spirit." (Ephesians 2:22) Thus the epistles confirmed that the New Testament church was established, and the content of these epistles clearly showed that the transition from law to grace was complete. (1 Corinthians 12:13) (Romans 8:9)

It would then be quite natural to expect to find, incorporated in these epistles, God's continuing program for dispensing His grace. Those procedures used by God for dispensing His grace during the period of transition were later discontinued or else superseded by permanent procedures ordained by God to continue in effect throughout the age of grace. These changes may be noted briefly with respect to the three items mentioned above as

follows:
1. THE BAPTISM OF THE HOLY SPIRIT

During the period of transition from law to grace three instances of the baptism of the Holy Spirit are recorded in the Book of Acts. The first instance occurred at a prayer meeting (Acts 1:14 & 2:1), the second at a preaching service (Acts 10:34-48), and the third at a ceremonial baptismal service (Acts 19:1-7) at Ephesus. Paul then stayed on at Ephesus for at least 2 years and 3 months and during this time wrote the first letter or epistle to the Corinthians. This epistle showed (1 Corinthians 12:13) that all believers had by then received the baptism of the Holy Spirit. And since this scripture, ever since it was written, has always applied to all true believers at all times, then it is obvious that the baptism of the Holy Spirit cannot now take place at anytime except at the moment of conversion. That all believers receive the Spirit at conversion is also confirmed by Romans 8:9.

2. SPEAKING IN TONGUES

At all three of the above instances of the baptism of the Holy Spirit, those who received the Holy Spirit spoke in other languages or tongues. This phenomenon of speaking in other languages or tongues first occurred on the day of Pentecost (Act 2:1-4). The purpose of this phenomenon on the day of Pentecost was to make it possible for everyone present to hear the gospel in his own native tongue. The purpose of this phenomenon on each of the other two of the three recorded instances of the baptism of the Holy Spirit was to supply convincing evidence that the Holy Spirit had been given in fundamentally the same way as on the day of Pentecost. As shown above, the baptism of the Holy Spirit always takes place now at the moment of conversion. Thus there is now no need of speaking in other languages or tongues to provide evidence of the baptism of the Holy Spirit. The scripture (rather than the speaking in tongues) now confirms that we Christians have all been baptized by the Holy Spirit. (1 Corinthians 12:13 and Romans 8:9)

Since there is no longer any need for the kind of tongues which accompanied the three instances of the baptism of the Holy Spirit recorded in the Book of Acts, and since there is no mention of this kind of tongues recurring anywhere after the occurrence at Ephesus in Acts 19:6, and since the requirement for an interpreter (1 Corinthians 14:27&28) prohibits any further spontaneous utterances in foreign languages in the church service, it seems necessary to conclude that this kind of tongues has ceased.

The kind of tongues referred to in 1 Corinthians, chapters 12:10 and 14:27&28, are distinctly different from the tongues in Acts 2:4, Acts 10:46, and Acts 19:6 in the following respects:

    A. The Tongues in the Book of Acts were the result of the instantaneous impulse of the Holy Spirit; those in 1 Corinthians 14:27&28 were not, for the number who were to be permitted to speak on any one occasion was to be limited to two or at the most three. (1 Corinthians 14:27) If the tongues in 1 Corinthians 14:27&28 had been the result of the instantaneous impulse of the Holy Spirit, then no limits would have been set, for the Scriptures do not set limits on the Holy Spirit.

    B. The tongues of 1 Corinthians, chapter 14:27&28 were gifts of the Holy Spirit whereas the tongues of Pentecost (Acts 2:4) as well as the tongues of Acts 10:46 and Acts 19:6 were not gifts of the Spirit but demonstrations of the Spirit. There is a decided difference between gifts of the Spirit and demonstrations of the Spirit. Gifts of the Spirit are permanent in nature and must be cultivated by the person who receives the gift. Demonstrations of the Holy Spirit are displays of the power of the Holy Spirit in which the Holy Spirit takes possession of a person's faculties for a limited period of time and uses them to accomplish a specific purpose.

We find illustrations in the scripture both of gifts of the Spirit and demonstrations of the Spirit. One of the best illustrations of a gift of the Spirit is seen in Paul's exhortations to the young preacher, Timothy. In his first letter to Timothy, Paul's exhortation in the 4th chapter, verse 14 is "Neglect not the gift that is in thee." And again in his second letter, chapter one and verse 6, Paul says "Wherefore I put thee in remembrance that thou stir up the gift of God, which is in thee by the putting on of my hands." And in the 2nd chapter, verse 15, Paul adds the practical exhortation "Study to show thyself approved unto God". Timothy was endowed by the Holy Spirit with the natural inclination and propensity for preaching, but it was necessary for him to cultivate this gift to realize his greatest potential.

Demonstrations of the Spirit do not require cultivation. The tongues on Pentecost, as we have noted, were a demonstration of the Holy Spirit. The virgin birth of our Saviour is another example. Saul prophesying in 1 Samuel 19:20-24 is another.

    C. The tongues of 1 Corinthians 14:27&28 differ from the tongues in Acts in that they require an interpreter whereas the tongues in the book of Acts did not require an interpreter.

    D. The tongues in Acts served as evidence of the baptism of the Holy Spirit, while the tongues in 1 Corinthians 14:27&28 did not serve as evidence of the baptism of the Spirit.

    E. The tongues in Acts are not valid for use in the church service whereas the tongues of 1 Corinthians 14:27&28 are. One reason the tongues in Acts are not valid is that they cannot conform to the requirement for an interpreter (1 Corinthians 14:27&28). By adding the requirement for an interpreter, God eliminated His approval of any further instances of spontaneous utterance in a foreign language in the church service. And it can readily be seen that if spontaneous utterances in real foreign languages could cause confusion in the church service, as Paul indicated in 1 Corinthians 14:26-33, then spontaneous utterances in synthetic syllables, such as charismatic tongues, would also cause confusion. And since God is not the author of confusion, charismatic tongues in the church service could hardly be ascribed to the Holy Spirit.

3. HEALING

It is generally recognized throughout the church that God can and does heal the physical body in accordance with His will. In both the Old Testament and the New Testament God has demonstrated His power to heal the body. We will concern ourselves with the part which the individual and the church play in God's program for dispensing His healing grace. Both the individual (who is endowed with the gift of healing) and the church play distinctly different roles in the realm of healing.

That God does give some individuals the gift of healing is shown in 1 Corinthians 12:28. However, it is necessary to understand that the gift of healing is *not* the power to work special miracles of healing. In Acts 19:11 we read that "God wrought special miracles by the hands of Paul." This does not say that Paul had the gift of healing nor the permanent ability to work special miracles of healing.

How do we conclude that Paul did not have the gift of healing when God had used him to work special miracles of healing as described in Acts 19:11? First, we must recognize that if Paul had had the gift of healing, it would have been permanent. This is clearly stated in Romans 11:29 where we read that "the gifts and calling of God are without repentance." And therefore, since the gifts of the Holy Spirit are permanent, the fact that Paul left Trophimus at Miletum sick (2 Timothy 4:20) shows that God had not endowed Paul with the ability to work miracles of healing. When "God wrought special miracles by the hands of Paul", it was the Holy Spirit demonstrating His healing power through Paul for a limited time.

It is a mistake to assume that the gift of healing is the power to work special miracles of healing. As the spectacular brilliance of the apostolic era was fading, authority to continue a program of healing by the power of God was transferred to the church according to the instructions given in James 5:14. And authority for the pursuit of a Christian vocation in healing was established by 1 Corinthians 12:28. And since the most important of the gifts of the Holy Spirit requires cultivation (2 Timothy 1:6), then the gift of healing would also require cultivation, for it would not be logical to expect miraculous power to accompany the lesser gifts while the most important (prophecy or preaching) relied on human effort. It is worth noting that Paul did not have the gift of healing, but God used him to work special miracles of healing. Luke, the physician, had the gift of healing, but there is no record of God using him to work special miracles of healing.

We may conclude these comments on the part which the individual plays in God's program for dispensing His healing grace by making a brief summary: The gifts of the Holy Spirit are those natural endowments which the Holy Spirit imparts to believers. These natural endowments are the abilities or talents which God entrusts to us to invest in the work of His kingdom as described in the parable in Matthew 25:14-28. If the gifts of the Spirit are confused with the demonstrations of the Spirit, believers then lose sight of the gifts of the Spirit which are theirs already. And instead of cultivating these gifts, they waste their lives seeking the power to duplicate the demonstrations of the Holy Spirit in healing and in tongues.

And likewise the church as a body may end up spending its time promoting its own brand of healing program instead of God's ordained way as given in James 5:14. But regarding the part which the church does play in God's program for dispensing His healing grace, we may make the following observations:

1. God does not give the gift of healing to the church. The gifts of the Holy Spirit are given to individuals.

2. Since the church does not possess the gift of healing, it is deceptive for the church to claim that it is a dispensary for God's healing grace except when the church follows the instructions given in James 5:14. But even when these instructions are followed, there is no guarantee that all who thus seek healing, will be healed. Those who claim that their church can guarantee that God will heal the body are either deceived or else they are imposters.

3. James 5:14 shows us that it is God's intent that, although His healing grace will be dispensed differently from Acts 5:15 and Acts 19:12, His healing ministry in the church is to continue. And further, this scripture puts the healing program of the church in a setting where it will *not* overshadow the preaching of the word. We are reminded by 1 Corinthians 12:28 that, with the passing of the apostolic era, the order of succession indicated by this verse elevates preaching and teaching to the place of primary importance for the church. This is in harmony with the Great Commission of Matthew 28:19&20.

It has been the purpose of these few brief paragraphs to show that certain special events which occurred in the period of transition from law to grace, as recorded in the Book of Acts, cannot serve as precedents for the activities of the New Testament church nor for the activities of individual believers. The pattern which the church is to follow in this age of grace in which we are living has been modified from the Old Testament pattern by the Gospels and by the inspired epistles to exclude the practices required (and some which were allowed) by the Mosaic code of law. And these same inspired epistles define the pattern of the church's activities to show that the instances of the baptism of the Holy Spirit, and of speaking in tongues, and of healing, as recorded in the Book of Acts, are not to be used as precedents for the church's activities.

Lack of understanding has resulted in a wrong emphasis on the activities of the Holy Spirit. This in turn has given rise to deceitful practices by some who have attempted to duplicate the demonstrations of the Holy Spirit as recorded in the Book of Acts. Some churches have even conducted classes on how to speak in tongues. False claims about healing have been made. And some believers have been labeled as inferior Christians because of their opposition to these errors.

These things have resulted in unchristian rivalry between churches and feelings of animosity between Christians at a time when the increasing activity of the advance echelons of Antichrist makes it imperative that every legitimate means be used to promote harmony and Christian love within the church. The messages to five of the seven churches mentioned in the second and third chapters of the Book of Revelation show that those doctrines and practices which are contrary to the Scriptures can only weaken and destroy the church. Now is the time when the church should be gathering its strength for the impending storm. If the church is to avail herself of the maximum strength which can be obtained through a spirit of Christian love, then it is imperative that we lay aside the errors of the charismatic way. And if we are to lay aside the errors of the charismatic way, it is necessary first to be able to recognize what those errors are.

To recognize what the charismatic errors are, we may begin by analyzing the term "charismatic." The term charismatic has its origin in the Greek word "charisma". Charisma means "grace, favor or kindness" and is usually translated as "gift". A charismatic person is one whose actions or abilities are supposed to result in part from certain "gifts". In a general sense the term "charismatic" means "gifted".

We may continue our analysis of the charismatic way by noting that there are some Christians who believe that it is possible to receive or attain

certain "gifts" which elevate them to spiritually superior status, and they sometimes refer to themselves as charismatics. The "gifts", which they claim to have received or attained, are usually one or more of the following:
1. The "gift" or the baptism of the Holy Spirit.
2. The "gift" of speaking in tongues.
3. The "gift" of healing.

As noted in several previous paragraphs, the Scriptures define the above "gifts" as spiritual realities. But a misunderstanding of what these "gifts" are has led many Christians into the errors of the charismatic way. The most common errors of the charismatic way are:
1. The belief that the baptism of the Holy Spirit occurs after conversion.
2. The belief that speaking in tongues is evidence of the baptism of the Holy Spirit.
3. The belief that God endows certain Christians with the power to perform miracles of healing as He did in the period of transition from law to grace.

Some Christians, who have been deceived into believing one or more of the above errors, have then claimed to have received one or more of the three previously listed "gifts". And then, to support such claims, some have resorted to deceptions of various kinds. And with the aid of such deceptions they have gained for themselves a reputation for being spiritually alive as did the church in Sardis (Revelation 3:1).

But the devastating effect of the charismatic way upon the church, and upon the home, and upon the spiritual lives of the unsuspecting is a mute warning to those who may be allured by the claim that the charismatic way leads to a more spiritual life and to more dedicated service to God. The charismatic way is a way of error which marches under the banner of truth. Their errors are camouflaged to appear similar to activities of the church during the period of transition from law to grace. Thus many are deceived into believing that the charismatic way is in harmony with the scriptures.

It is sometimes supposed that, since some charismatics preach Christ, their errors are of little consequence. The messages to two of the seven churches (Revelation 2:12&18) illustrate the consequences of false doctrine within the church. And those consequences are not diminished by good works or charity or service or faith (Revelation 2:13&19).

To escape the errors of the charismatic way, a reasonable knowledge of the Scriptures is important. But one need not be drawn into the errors of that way while attaining a knowledge of the Scriptures. Following the truths which the Holy Spirit reveals to us day by day as we read and study God's word will keep us from the path of error. Truth is the remedy for error, and we have the promise of John 16:13 — "But when He, the Spirit of truth, is come, He will guide you into all truth —".

The words of the great hymn by Marcus Wells provide a beautiful summary of the comfort and assurance which the Holy Spirit supplies to Christians:

> *Holy Spirit, faithful Guide,*
> *Ever near the Christian's side;*
> *Gently lead us by the hand,*
> *Pilgrims in a desert land;*
> *Weary souls forever rejoice,*
> *While they hear that sweetest voice,*
> *Whispering softly, "Wanderer, come!*
> *Follow me, I'll guide thee home."*

Failure to follow the guidance of the Holy Spirit, as He illuminates the Holy Scriptures, adds unnecessary grief and difficulty to the Christian life and diminishes the efficiency of the church in the task of fulfilling the Great Commission. But nevertheless, God will accomplish His will. God has ordained that the old creation (the entire physical creation, both animate and inanimate) will bear the scars of Adam's sin. In the old creation "God created man in His own image." (Genesis 1:27) The new creation changes mortals to new creatures in Christ. (2 Corinthians 5:17) And in that day when our weeping is ended (Revelations 21:4), and the old creation is no more, the effects of original sin will no longer blind our eyes to the purpose and plan of God. And then we will be able to see that God's will to save every soul has been accomplished. For God "worketh all things after the counsel of His own will." (Ephesians 1:11) God cannot fail. Jesus said "— with God all things are possible." (Matthew 19:26)

Fragments of The Future

LIFE'S JOURNEY

If you are a pilgrim on some fearful journey,
And the sky seems all gloomy and black,
And the dangers you know are before you,
All say that you ought to turn back,
And your friends like Job's comforters tell you:
Your courage is only an act;
Ignore their well-meaning counsel
And think on this notable fact
All of the storms are on this side of Jordan,
And heaven is always intact.

David E. Bower 1985

THE DUSTY ROAD

"Dust to dust returneth"
And dost thou ask, For why?
For dust is Extra baggage,
When you're headed for the sky.

Dust to dust returneth
Nor can this mortal sigh,
For though I'm spent and weary
I am headed for the sky.

Dust to dust returneth
The trumpet sounds on high.
The graves of saints are opened,
And they're headed for the sky.

Dust to dust returneth
Are you sure you'll never die?
Before thy summons cometh
Start heading for the sky.

Dust to dust returneth
No longer ask, For why?
When Jesus grants you pardon,
You are headed for the sky.

David E. Bower 1985

EXIT TO ETERNITY

The flickering light and the creaking door
And the silence that echoes forevermore,
These pervade the halls of death
And testify of fleeting breath.
The trembling voice and pallid brow
Confirm that soon the time is now.

Death has for us no strong appeal
Nor joyful sound nor earnest zeal.
Death lingers near the battle cry
Not warning that the time is nigh

Life has for all one sure appointment
Neither stench nor fragrant ointment.
Appointed not to sing or sigh
Just appointed "once to die".

Death does not serve to set us free
For death is our last enemy.
Death forbids our flesh and blood
To walk upon the streets of gold.

By consequence of Adam's sin
These bodies cannot enter in.
Nor is death a chastening rod
To make us fit to live with God

Death sets the stage that saints may be
Like Jesus in eternity,
Standing on the crystal sea
And clothed with immortality

David E. Bower 1994

CREATION
OLD AND NEW

Sing a song of glory
While heaven's praises roll
When God displayed His image
Making dust a living soul.

Sing a song of Adam
With intellect refined
Transplanted in the Garden
And perfectly designed.

Sing a song of helpers
For Adam none was found
Till Adam's rib was taken
And Eve was brought around.

Sing a song of Satan
Who chills the heart and mind
Excelling in deception
To make the spirit blind.

Sing a song of tragedy
When Eve put forth her hand
And Adam's error made the earth
A dark and dismal land.

Sing a song of sacred art
That illustrates man's sinful heart:
When God ordains that life begin
He paints the scars of Adam's sin.

Sing a song of hate and greed
That rules the human race
And dims the grandeur of the day
When clay became a human face.

Sing a song of sinners
Degraded and defiled
Condemning their Creator
Whose word they had reviled.

Sing a song of crosses
Erected on a hill
Where creatures and Creator
Will destiny fulfill.

Sing a song of terror
When darkness filled the land
And Satan smote his hollow breast
And said, The victroy's mine.

Sing a song of spices
With linen clothes and myrrh
And a tomb within a garden
Where none was known to stir.

Sing a song of silence
While soldiers guard the dead
And tremble as the stone is moved
For courage now has fled.

Sing a song of triumph
While the hosts of Satan flee
For Christ has conquered sin and death
And set the captives free.

Sing a song of mortals
Compelled by love divine
To taste the hidden manna
And say, Salvation's mine.

Sing a song of gladness
That lasts forevermore
When, to a man, the fallen race
Will meet on heaven's shore

David E. Bower 1995

AN EXHORTATION

Let no one suppose that the conclusions set forth in the previous pages provide any reason for any one to believe that to engage in good works is optional. For "faith without works is dead". (James 2:20) God uses good works to keep our faith active. God uses good works to increase our faith. God uses good works to build His kingdom. Thus "we are labourers together with God". (1 Corinthians 3:9) Thus we lay up "treasures in heaven". (Matthew 6:20) And whether it is a kind word or a cold cup of water, every effort has its reward. For Jesus said, "Inasmuch as ye have done it unto one of the least of these my brethren, ye have done it unto Me." (Matthew 25:40) And just as we are exhorted to "be careful to maintain good works" (Titus 3:8), we are also exhorted to go "into all the world, and preach the gospel to every creature". (Mark 16:15) And although the Lord is "not willing that any should perish" (2 Peter 3:9) and "worketh all things after the counsel of His own will" (Ephesians 1:11) so that not even one soul will be lost, yet He offers to each of us the high privilege of labouring together with Him in publishing the gospel throughout the world. Jesus said, "The harvest truly is great, but the labourers are few" (Luke 10:2). Let us then respond to God's call and labour together with Him. Let us respond in our own places in each situation as the prophet Isaiah did when he said, "Here am I; send me." (Isaiah 6:8) And then one day, along with the prophet Isaiah and the saints of the ages, we shall hear those welcome words, "Well done thou good and faithful servant.". (Matthew 25:21) And until that day we shall have the same testimony as Enoch: "that he pleased God.". (Hebrews 11:5) And also, we shall have the rewards that accumulate to those who obey the exhortation to lay up "treasures in heaven". (Matthew 6:20)